# SIBERIAN VILLAGE

PUBLISHED IN COOPERATION WITH THE CENTER FOR AMERICAN PLACES

*Santa Fe, New Mexico · Harrisonburg, Virginia*

# SIBERIAN VILLAGE

## LAND AND LIFE IN THE SAKHA REPUBLIC

*Bella Bychkova Jordan*
*Terry G. Jordan-Bychkov*

UNIVERSITY OF MINNESOTA PRESS
*Minneapolis · London*

The University of Minnesota Press gratefully acknowledges financial assistance provided by the University of Texas, Austin, in support of this publication.

Portions of chapter 5 appeared in an earlier version as "Post-Soviet Change in a Yakutian Farm Village" by Bella Bychkova Jordan, Terry G. Jordan-Bychkov, and Robert K. Holz, in *Erdkunde* 52, no. 3 (1998): 219–31; reprinted here with permission.

Published by the University of Minnesota Press
111 Third Avenue South, Suite 290
Minneapolis, MN 55401-2520
http://www.upress.umn.edu

A Cataloging-in-Publication record for this book is available from the Library of Congress.
ISBN 0-8166-3569-2

Printed in the United States of America on acid-free paper
The University of Minnesota is an equal-opportunity educator and employer.

11  10  09  08  07  06  05  04  03  02  01          10  9  8  7  6  5  4  3  2  1

TO OLGA DANILOVNA TIKHONOVA, 1938–1998

# CONTENTS

# LIST OF ILLUSTRATIONS

# ACKNOWLEDGMENTS

In acquiring such a wealth of information about Djarkhan and its place in Sakha-Yakutia, we received assistance of many kinds from the people of the village and republic. Truly, the book would have not been written had these good people not helped us.

Above all, many residents of Djarkhan opened their homes, hearts, and minds to us, eager to have the story of their beloved village told. In particular, we are indebted to Arkady Ivanov, head of the Djarkhan Village Council; to Vladimir Kondratiev, independent peasant farmer; Afanasy Myreyev, leader of the main agricultural cooperative at the village; Tanya Tikhonova, who fed us and offered the use of her *banya*; Aleksandra Tikhonova, schoolteacher who took winter photographs of the village; Moisey Ivanov, who told us many stories; Zinaida Popova, songwriter and schoolteacher; Vasily Tikhonov, a fine companion; Yuri and Lana Tikhonov and their respective families, who hosted a second wedding party for us in the village; Okdos Pakhomova; and the many others who extended us the warmest hospitality. Salt of the earth, one and all. May you live one hundred years and your village endure forever.

In Suntar, the county seat, Liya Savvinova made room for us in her beautiful home and fed us like royalty. Ksenia Ammonsova did likewise in her wonderful old log house, plying us with *suorat,* red currant juice, and other delicacies. Semyon Zedgenizov opened the door to the governor's office and swam with us in Grandfather Vilyui, among other favors, while Nikolai Petrov drove us to and from Djarkhan, no small service in the absence of any public transportation or car rental service. Georgiy Yakovlev, governor of Suntar Ulus, kindly assisted us by having the archives opened for us during the official vacation period, providing access to previously classified maps, and offering the services of a car and driver. Lyudmila Petrovna, director of the archive, and her knowledgeable assistant, Arkady Yakovlev, provided essential data, taking time away from their vacation to do so.

Innokentiy Pakhomov of Yakutsk, head of the Sakha Republic Committee for Land Reform and a Djarkhan native, went with us into the field numerous times, providing a vehicle and driver (and even Lena River boats), allowing us to see diverse other agricultural villages in all directions from Yakutsk, a useful comparison that put Djarkhan in perspective. He shared with us his knowledge and wisdom about the post-Soviet period. His influence, if not always cited, appears throughout the book. What fine times we had with him in the three great valleys, in the *alases* east of the Lena, and on the river. He is a gentleman and a scholar.

Also in Yakutsk, we are indebted to Mikhail Ivanov, Sakha's toponymic expert, a living cultural treasure of the republic, for sharing his extensive knowledge with us. Matriona Zacharova, who presides over the remarkable collection of rare books at the Yakutsk municipal library, was most helpful, fetching scores of dusty old volumes and allowing us unrestricted access to the collection's priceless Middendorff, all the while dealing with Terry in fluent German. She is a credit to her profession.

Gail Fondahl, a Siberian specialist and geographer at the University of Northern British Columbia, brought our attention to the neotraditionalist literature and generously photocopied for our use her copy of the fugitive book by Pika and Prokhorov. Professor Robert K. Holz of the Department of Geography at the University of Texas gave us support and advice when we needed it most, and he will always have a special place in our hearts. The late Paul

Ward English, of the same department, read an early draft of the manuscript and provided many useful suggestions, as did Victor L. Arnold of the School of Business at the University of Texas. Vic is also the one who brought Bella to the university from Sakha, and without his help, none of this would ever have happened. If we ever have sons, we will name them for Vic and Bob! Gregory Knapp, chairman of the Department of Geography, also provided timely support and guidance that we appreciated very much.

Chauncy Harris, professor emeritus of geography at the University of Chicago and a famed Russian specialist, generously provided his file copies of the two reports by Terence Armstrong, listed in the references. Just try finding those reports sometime! Professor Victor L. Mote, a geographer at the University of Houston and preeminent Siberian specialist, read the manuscript and made many suggestions for its improvement, providing at the same time his enthusiastic encouragement and support, for which we are most grateful. He also shared with us his own field observations from 1985, when he became the first foreigner ever to visit the Vilyui Bend country.

John Cotter, a master cartographer, drafted the beautiful maps in the book. We were fortunate to have his services. Kelly Hobbs typed the manuscript cheerfully and superbly, coping with the gibberish of transliterated Russian and Yakutian without complaint or error. We have never proofread cleaner copy.

A preliminary, simplified version of chapter 5 was published earlier in the German geographical journal *Erdkunde* (Jordan et al. 1998); we are grateful to the editors of that journal for the resultant professional exposure and scholarly feedback, as well as for their permission to incorporate certain materials from the article in the present book.

Our greatest debt is to George F. Thompson, president of the Center for American Places in Harrisonburg, Virginia, who enthusiastically supported us in this endeavor from the original idea through the book proposal and the process of finding the best publisher (a goal he attained most impressively). We are grateful for George's encouragement, knowledge, and skill. For a decade and a half, George has been our friend, counselor, confidant, and supporter. *Siberian Village* is the third of our books to be published through his Center, and we look forward to continued association with him. George deserves the gratitude of the entire discipline for his labors on behalf of cultural geography. *Spasibo bolshoye,* George!

Finally, we dedicate this book to Bella's late mother, Olga Danilovna Tikhonova (1938–1998). Olga, a daughter of Djarkhan, brought honor to her native place through her distinguished medical career in the wider world. Warm, loving, vivacious, intelligent, and accomplished, she died all too young. She served as our unfailing authority on all matters concerning the village, and we consulted with her often. A dear mother and a precious mother-in-law, she is much missed, and this book is as much hers as ours. Rest in peace, you who leaped the chasm between parallel worlds.

# 1 · SIBERIA: MYTH AND REALITY

Deep in the boreal forests of subarctic Asia, a hardy people—the Yakuts, or Sakhalar as they call themselves—wrest a living from an unforgiving polar land as sedentary cattle and horse raisers. They carried this ancient Eurasian livelihood farther poleward than any other people, a remarkable feat, considering the extreme severity of the regional climate. The Sakhalar reside in sizable permanent villages, the northernmost such agrarian settlements in the world, perched on the very outermost margins of the agricultural habitat in Eurasia.

Our book concerns one such village, a representative Yakut settlement named Djarkhan. We endeavor to present a portrait of this place, an image of land and life in a remote locale as it has evolved over the past three to four centuries. To do so, we employ the perspective and methods of geography, the academic discipline concerned with places and human adaptation to the natural habitat.

## LAND OF MYTH

Our village lies in a fabled land, Siberia, and more exactly in the autonomous Republic of Sakha-Yakutia, a part of Russia's Far East province (Map 1.1). If we are to comprehend this village, we must first consider the vast region and republic to which it belongs. The name *Siberia*, to both Russians and foreigners, comes laden with meaning, myth, and mystery. The very etymology of the name remains uncertain, though the toponym probably—and improbably—derives from a tiny splinter principality of the collapsed Mongol Empire situated in the extreme southwestern corner of the present Siberia.[1] The Russians, moving eastward to conquer and colonize these lands beyond the Urals, carried the name *Sibir* with them all the way to the Pacific and Arctic shores, making something vast of what had been small.

The relatively few people who traveled in Siberia before 1900 wrote fascinating accounts of exotic surroundings and peoples, but the huge region remained largely unknown. Even in the early twentieth century, a few privileged Western explorers still plumbed Siberia's depths.[2] Myths develop easily out of such ignorance, to fill in the blank spaces on maps.

On one level, Siberia represents the Russian equivalent of the American West. Both are huge, mythical, thinly populated regions lying on the peripheries of their respective megastates. Both remain in some measure frontier districts today, rich in resources, places to get a new start in life or to perish. Both are regions of "unbridled Nature," of great physical beauty and visual splendor, breathtaking to behold, but afflicted with difficult climates that require special human adaptations.[3] Both are lands of profound variety, though the internal contrasts lie hidden beneath the stereotypes of myth. In this sense, both Siberia and the West are more impressive in reality than in the myths associated with them. Both possess vast natural resources that have been mindlessly and wastefully exploited without being exhausted, and Siberia remains even today "a promised land of frozen milk and honey."[4]

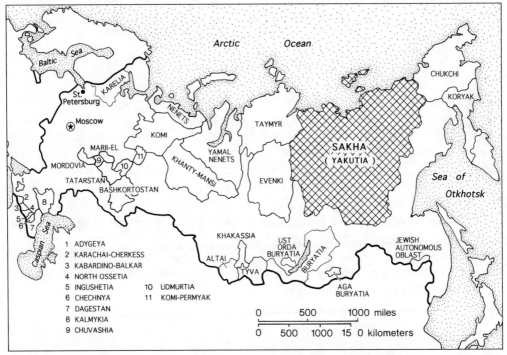

Map 1.1. *Russia and its major ethnic subdivisions. Sakha-Yakutia is the largest of the ethnic republics.* (Sources: *Harris 1993, 550; Espenshade, Hudson, and Morrison 1995, 166–67.*)

But, such comparisons aside, Siberia also differs from any other place on Earth. "Virtually a continent in its own right," the region is simply vast.[5] It is also remote, allowing deeper and more mythic meanings and messages than the American West possesses. For some, Siberia connotes a land of exile, struggle, punishment, imprisonment, and death in a brutally cold climate. Siberia housed Aleksandr Solzhenitsyn's Gulag Archipelago, the Soviet refinement of the older, czarist practice of banishment.[6] Human suffering surely provides part of the complex and often contradictory perception of Siberia. A German visitor wrote, over a century ago, that Siberia to the European "is a land of fright, of endless forests, deserts, hostile climate, and criminalized people," an image he then contradicted with his own firsthand observations of "wondrous beauty," healthful climates, and contented natives.[7] To one Russian writer, the name *Siberia* sounds "like a warning bell announcing something vaguely powerful." God, it is said, designed Siberia at the end of Creation, when he had begun "to have doubts about the human race."[8] In the English language, *Siberia* can mean "any undesirable or isolated locale or job to which one is assigned as punishment or a mark of disfavor."[9]

Until very recently, Siberia remained largely closed to outsiders. In fact, a coauthor of this book was the first American ever to set foot in Djarkhan village, in 1997, and then only because he had married a native of the place, his coauthor. Only five other foreign-born persons had preceded him there, three of whom were Mongols. As a consequence of its inaccessibility, Siberia acquired the aura of mystery that is inevitably attached to forbidden places. Rumors and legends about this region circulated for centuries before Russia actually seized it. At some symbolic level, people have always filled such unattainable places with strange and fantastic creatures on their mental maps. Sometimes these dragons witness startling events, such as, the great mysterious explosion in the early 1900s in the impenetrable heart of the Siberian forests that leveled huge expanses of woodland in the Ust'-Tunguska River region. Fragmentary stories filter out about such remarkable events, adding to the sense of mystery and providing Siberia "an irresistible and disquieting attraction."[10]

Part of the meaning and romance of Siberia also derives from its role as a meeting ground of the world's two greatest civilizations—Europe and Asia.[11] Because the two meet and mingle here, Siberia necessarily seems exotic to adherents of both of those cultures, assuming in the process its own special identity.[12] For several centuries, "the place of Asia in the Russian mind" has centered in part upon Siberia.[13]

To the native peoples of Siberia, including the inhabitants of Djarkhan village, the mystery and mythology have a very different source. For them, Siberia is not foreign, stigmatized, peripheral, forbidding, or exotic, but instead familiar, inviting, and central, as only a homeland can be. These people bear a highly emotional attachment to their native place and region.[14] Land and life here are so inseparable as to become a single entity, and the Siberians' sense of mystery comes from the nature spirits that inhabit their forests, waters, winds, and skies—shamanistic forces not completely extinguished by centuries of Orthodox Christian missionary work and decades of pervasive Soviet atheistic ideology. In some measure, shamanism reflects a hard land. Siberian regional mysticism derives in no small part from the endless endeavor to wrest a living from a very demanding and unforgiving environment. Survival is precarious here, and nature's potent spirits must be appeased.

To foreigner and native alike, then, Siberia seems at once mysterious, fascinating, terrifying, awesome, beautiful, exotic, familiar, and mythic. Small wonder that its very name evokes complex and at times contradictory images or emotions. But what are the realities of the region that both underlie and defy its mythology?

## SIBERIAN REALITY

Siberian realities, stripped of myth, are less romantic but still impressive. Its vastness is real, as are its resource wealth, tortured history, and emptiness. But Siberia is also a land where Diet Coke, cyberpleasures, opera, and ballet coexist with largely traditional native cultures. The modern age has left a deep imprint on this land, and "nowadays going to Siberia is no great feat," but the traditional ways of life abundantly survive. A journey from Moscow to Yakutsk, capital of the present Republic of Sakha-Yakutia, took one year in 1650, one hundred days in 1820, and only six hours today, but many parts of Siberia remain rather isolated. A "friction of distance" persists in Siberia that confounds the visitor.[15]

Since our village, Djarkhan, lies in Sakha-Yakutia, let us seek Siberian realities within the boundaries of that republic (Map 1.2). Sakha well reflects the true character of the entire region, not surprising since the republic encompasses fully one-fourth of Siberia, containing more than three million square kilometers, or about 1.2 million square miles. This huge republic accounts for nearly a fifth of Russia's land area and is two-fifths the size of Australia or the contiguous continental United States (Map 1.3). Often described as "Russia's Alaska," Sakha in fact comes close to twice the size of that largest American state. The republic spans approximately 2,500 kilometers, or 1,550 miles, in east-west dimension, including three

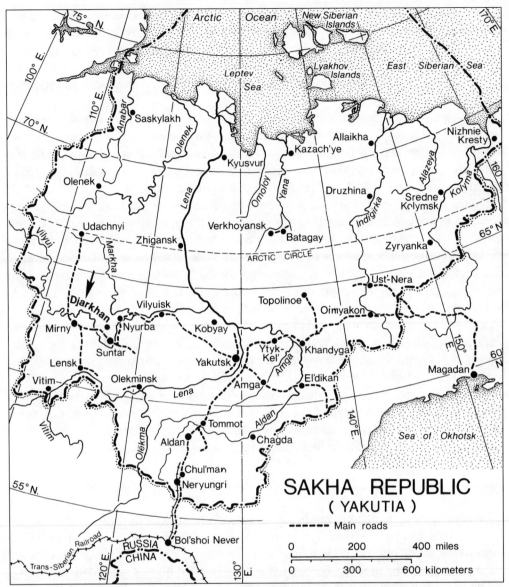

Map 1.2. *General locations in the Sakha Republic.* (Sources: *"Russia: Eastern Part"* 1996; *"Yakutskaya ASSR"* 1934.)

time zones and fifty-seven degrees of longitude—nearly one-sixth of the earth's circumference at this high latitude. The republic stretches some 2,000 kilometers, or 1,250 miles south-to-north, from 55° 30' to 76° latitude, and 40 percent of its territory lies north of the Arctic Circle. Sakha, though mainly continental in location, has a lengthy coastline on the great frozen polar sea and includes several sizable oceanic islands. Areally, it is by far the largest of Russia's twenty-one ethnic republics.[16]

Sakha's spectacular geographical dimensions stand in profound contrast to its unimpressive population size. Only slightly more than a million inhabitants live in the republic —about 0.3 persons per square kilometer (0.83 per square mile). Sakha accounts for only 3 percent of Siberia's people and a mere 0.7 percent of the population of Russia. Just

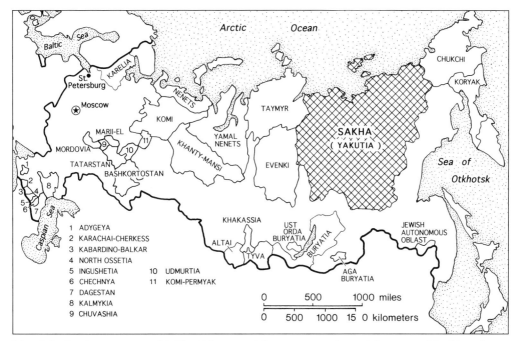

Map 1.3. *Areal comparison of Sakha-Yakutia and the contiguous forty-eight states of the United States. The latitudes, of course, are not comparable.*

under two-thirds of all residents—64 percent—live in urban places, including the capital, Yakutsk, with 196,500 people. Ten other cities and towns have over ten thousand inhabitants, in addition to sixty-eight smaller "urban settlements." Rural areas have only one person for every 8.5 square kilometers (3.3 square miles).[17] Djarkhan village, then, is a profoundly rural place.

As recently as 1917, over 95 percent of Yakutia's people lived in rural settlements, but the Soviet period witnessed a near quadrupling of the population, linked to immigration and rapid urbanization. Between 1979 and 1989 alone, the republic's population increased by almost 29 percent. Today Sakha is one of the few parts of Russia where natural population increase continues, if very modestly, though a high emigration rate has recently caused a decline in the total population, from its peak of 1,109,000 in 1991 to 976,400 by 2000. However, the total fertility rate plummeted from 2.4 in 1989 to 1.9 in 1996, portending eventual natural decline. The infant mortality rate—perhaps the single best indicator of living standards—stood at 18.9 per thousand in 1989 and 19.1 in 1997, satisfactory by world standards. Life expectancy at birth in 1999 was 65 years in Sakha, with a startling difference between males, at 60, and females, at 70.[18]

## ETHNIC GROUPS

Sakha's million inhabitants are unevenly divided among no fewer than 80 nationality groups. Principal among them are the Russians, who make up less than 45 percent of the population, and the Sakhalar or Yakuts, the Turkic-speaking titular group in the republic, who number 380,000 there and form over 40 percent of the total number of inhabitants today.[19] The remaining minorities consist in part of other nationalities derived from the European part of

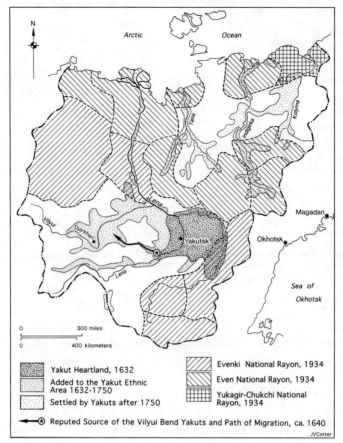

Map 1.4. *Sakha-Yakutia, showing the spread of the Sakhalar after the arrival of the Russians in 1632 and the peripheral homelands of the more ancient inhabitants of the Republic. The Yakut heartland lies in the Central Yakut Plain. Djarkhan village lies in the expanded Yakut Heartland, an area settled after 1632. Evenkia, peripheral to the Yakut heartland, remained the stronghold of the Evenks. In 1989, the Even-Bytantaisk ethnic rayon was added, as were others in the 1990s (not shown on map). (Sources: Slezkine 1994, xv–xvi; Forsyth 1992, 285; Milner-Gulland and Dejevsky 1989, 26–27; Jochelson 1934, 220–25; Fondahl 1993, 499.)*

the country, most notably Ukrainians. The Russians and other Europeans live mainly in urban centers, leaving the countryside, including Djarkhan, very largely Yakut. The Evenks (Tungus) and Evens, Mongolic peoples believed to be of Manchurian origin, and diverse other ancient Siberian groups, in particular the Yukagirs and Chukchis, also represent the native population (Map 1.4). By the 1600s, when the Russians arrived, the Sakhalar lived along the middle Lena River, while Evenks and Evens held the peripheral lands. In 1632, the Russians officially incorporated Yakutia, as they call it, into their state.[20]

After the Revolution of 1917, the Bolshevik government declared that every national or ethnic group in Russia had a right to political recognition and status. While Lenin viewed ethnic assimilation as progressive and inevitable, he wanted to appease national minorities by extending rights denied in czarist times, in the hope they would support the Revolution.

In the first Soviet Constitution, fifteen large cultural and ethnic groups received first-rank status as Soviet Republics.[21] Lower-ranking tiers of ethnic administrative units for less populous groups were also created, including, among others, Autonomous Soviet Socialist Republics, and national *rayons*. Sakha achieved, in the early 1920s, second-tier status as the Yakutian Autonomous Soviet Socialist Republic, while Evenks, Evens, Chukchis, and Yukagirs were awarded national *rayons* within the Yakutian ASSR (Map 1.4).[22]

This complicated system of ethnic political organization masked the true Soviet ideology —that the population of the USSR would become homogenized in the course of time, both ethnically and culturally. In fact, a policy of Russification was soon implemented beneath the outward celebration of ethnic variety. Russification accompanied an "internal colonialism," in a classical core-periphery manner. "Nationalist deviation" became one of the counterrevolutionary crimes in the Soviet Union.[23]

Under this system Yakutia remained an internal colony of the Soviet Slavic core, just as it had been in czarist times, though Moscow heavily subsidized the resource exploitation.[24] Most factory-made goods were imported to the republic, while raw materials dominated the exports. Sakha's dependence was not merely economic, for it also had to follow directives from Moscow concerning education and cultural development. More crucially, Slavic immigrants came in large numbers to Yakutia, causing the percentage of ethnic Sakhalar in the republic's population to drop from an 82 percent majority in 1926, when 241,000 Yakuts lived in the republic, to a 46 percent minority by 1959, by which time their numbers had fallen to 233,000. As a result of Russification, a sizable segment of a whole generation of Yakuts today does not properly know its own language and history, though 94 percent of all Sakhalar still speak their ancestral tongue. Even remote Djarkhan was not spared Russification. Beginning in 1967, for example, all secondary-school instruction in the Yakutian ASSR had to be in Russian, even in the villages.[25]

The Sakha Republic's status changed in a dramatic way in 1990, when it achieved the status of a full republic and adopted a declaration of state sovereignty. According to this document, Sakha became a sovereign, democratic, law-governed state within the Russian Federation, with its own government, headed by a president and parliament. The legislative power resides in two chambers of the Legislative Assembly of Sakha. In diverse ways, the people of Sakha have demonstrated distinctive political tendencies. A mild form of ethnonationalism can be said to exist in the republic today. It remains to be seen how much genuine autonomy Sakha and other republics will be able to maintain within Russia, though one expert labeled Sakha a "state within a state." Following the economic crisis of 1998, the outlying provinces became more dependent on Moscow.[26]

The Republic of Sakha-Yakutia, as it is now called, has its own flag, showing the white Arctic sun against a blue background, and an official state emblem featuring an image of a horseback rider taken from the ancient cave art of Yakutia. The addition of the name *Sakha* represents a significant change. *Yakutia*, bestowed by the Russians, is perceived by the republic's titular group as a legacy of cultural colonialism. *Sakha* is the traditional Yakut name both for themselves and their land.[27]

In the middle 1990s, 72 percent of all Sakhalar identified themselves primarily as citizens of Sakha rather than Russia, a sentiment also expressed by a third of all ethnic Russians living in the republic. An additional 24 percent of Yakuts and 36 percent of ethnic Russians expressed equal loyalty to Sakha and Russia. Secession seems unlikely, and two-thirds of the Yakuts in 1994 described the ethnic situation as "calm," as did a majority of the local Russians. Certainly that adjective describes the situation in Djarkhan village. Ethnic violence, which erupted in Yakutsk between Russians and Sakhalar in 1979 and 1986, has not recurred. In the 1990s, many thousands of Russians emigrated from Sakha-Yakutia, more for economic than political reasons, allowing the titular group to increase their proportion of the republic's total population.[28]

In the Federal Treaty of 1992 and Bilateral Treaty of 1995, coupled with several other agreements, Russia awarded Sakha a real measure of political autonomy and economic independence. The republic acquired the right to manage its mineral resources. Under the new system, Sakha did not just send its diamonds, gold, and other natural resources to Moscow, but instead sold them to Russia. Moreover, 26 percent of all rough diamonds and 30 percent of gold mined in the republic could be sold by Sakha directly to foreign customers.[29] In the late 1990s, this privilege eroded, and little mineral wealth now goes directly to Sakha. The republic can prohibit nuclear weapons testing or placement of nuclear weapons in its territory and ban all nuclear explosions used for mining or geological purposes. The Sakhalar remember all too well the massive radioactive fallout that doused the republic in 1961 as a result of a Soviet hydrogen bomb test on the Russian Arctic island of Novaya Zemyla, causing long-term health problems, not to mention twelve subsequent underground bomb tests carried out on Sakha's territory. Further evidence of the republic's autonomy is seen in Sakha's negotiated right to keep a larger share of collected tax revenues than most other republics and its refusal on three different occasions to send even this smaller amount of tax revenue to Moscow. The Russian government, in response, has threatened and implemented cutbacks in federally financed programs.[30]

Sakha enjoys independent economic and cultural relations with a number of foreign countries. The republic established relations at an official level with Latvia, Mongolia, South Korea, China, and Slovenia. Intergovernmental cooperation has been established with Kazakstan, Ukraine, and some republics within the Russian Federation. To participate in the international political process, Sakha joined UNESCO and the Organization of Unrepresented Nations and Peoples.[31] It belongs to the Northern Forum, an international advocacy group for northern regions and countries. The republic also has a trade office in Tokyo and seeks to become more actively engaged in the economy of the "Pacific rim."[32] This effort has been hampered recently by the economic malaise of East Asia.

## HABITAT

In its effort to become more integrated into the world economy, Sakha Republic is handicapped by physical geography. Sakhans must cope with a severe climate, difficult terrain, and peripheral location. And the republic is walled off from the Pacific shore by rugged mountains and virtually landlocked, since the Arctic Coast remains frozen most of the year.

The most remarkable aspect of the Yakutian environment without question is the climate. To outsiders visiting Sakha, at least, the astounding temperatures leave no doubt concerning their personal smallness and vulnerability. The severity of Siberia's climate contributes to its image as an exotic and harsh land. In December and January, temperatures can drop into the range of −60° to −70° centigrade (−76° to −94°F), and the high valleys and plateaus between the mountain ranges of northeastern Sakha experience coldness almost beyond imagination. The towns there vie for the title of the coldest inhabited place on earth.

Throughout Sakha, winter month averages in the −40° to −50°C (−40° to −58°F) range are not uncommon. In the brief summer season, temperatures between 30° to 38°C (86° to 100°F) are experienced, buoyed by the lengthy duration of sunlight and "white nights." The July average at the capital, Yakutsk, is 19°C (66°F). Sakha has the largest annual temperature range in the world, with a difference of over 56°C (100°F) between the warmest and coldest months. The profound continentality of the climate derives from the republic's location on the world's largest landmass, surrounded by mountain ranges and an ice-covered northern sea. The fact that the Arctic Ocean is perpetually frozen not only robs Sakha of the mitigating effects of marine thermal influences, but also transforms that same sea into a spawning ground of bitterly cold air masses.[33]

Annual precipitation totals are very modest, usually in the range of 200 to 300 millimeters (8 to 12 inches). Aridity is avoided only because low temperatures retard evaporation. Russian meteorologists apply the term *dry microthermal* to the republic's climate.[34] Most of Sakha lies in the zone of extreme subarctic climate, with the coldest month averaging below −38°C (−36°F) and a pronounced winter dry season, caused by very high barometric pressure and absence of marine influences.[35] All of Sakha is included in the boreal belt of permafrost, in which the subsurface remains eternally frozen. In some places the permafrost reaches very great depths, and during the summer months, the ground thaws only to a depth of 0.4 to 3.5 meters (1.3 to 11.5 feet).[36]

Sakha's terrain consists of expansive plateaus, rugged folded mountain ranges, and broad lowlands (Map 1.5). In the heart of the republic is the Central Yakut Plain, where nine-tenths of the people live, including the villagers of Djarkhan.[37] The plain, studded with countless small lakes, is a huge tectonic sink, a downfolding of the earth's crust at the western foot of the towering, upfolded Verhoyansk Range. On the other three sides, the Central Yakut Plain is flanked by expansive plateaus that dominate southern and western Sakha, standing generally at an elevation of 500 to 700 meters (1,650 to 2,300 feet) above sea level. These uplands, deeply incised by various rivers, form part of the Central Siberian Plateau, one of the largest landform regions on the face of the earth. To the east the heavily glaciated, folded mountain complexes wall off the republic from the Pacific coast.[38]

Sakha, including the region around Djarkhan village, is largely a realm of the *taiga,* the boreal coniferous forest that occupies 72 percent of its territory. The Yakutian *taiga* appears at first glance as an endless, contiguous ocean of green, but in some areas, especially the Central Yakut Plain, one sees small grassy openings and elongated, grass-filled stream valleys. These grasslands interrupt the monotony of the overwhelming arboreal dark green. Djarkhan lies in the midst of such grassy openings. The seeming monotony of forest also conceals a huge variety of nonarboreal plants, such as eighty-five different medicinal herbs, diverse wild berries, and mushrooms. In the northern part of Sakha, and in the mountain ranges, beyond the treeline in the coldest areas, lies a huge expanse of tundra, a treeless land of grasses, sedges, and moss.[39]

Sakha's wildlife has always been a major resource for livelihood. Animals provided the natives with food, clothes, tools, and even building material for traditional houses. In spite of the harsh environment, Sakha's fauna is diverse. There are 64 species of mammals and 280 of birds. Among the most important are valuable fur animals, represented by 20 species, including the sable, ermine, and Arctic fox and squirrel, the abundance and high quality of which make Sakha the largest fur producer in Russia. In different parts of the republic

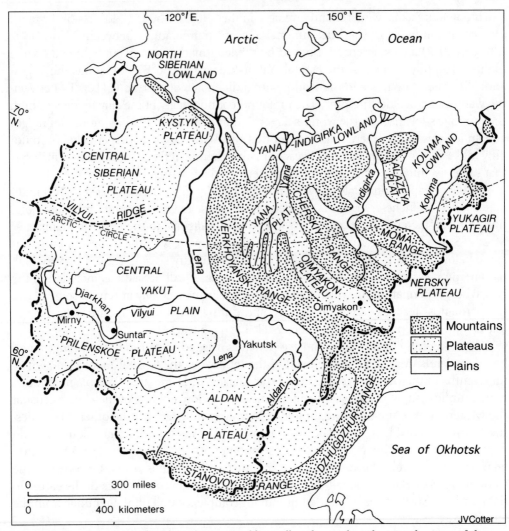

Map 1.5. *Terrain regions of Sakha-Yakutia. Djarkhan village lies in the Vilyui Bend section of the Central Yakut Plain, in the expanded Yakut Heartland.* (Sources: *Suslov 1961, 210–11; Berg 1950, 362; "Russia: Eastern Part" 1996.*)

are also ranges for elk, bighorn sheep, the longhaired Yakutian pony, and wild reindeer—numbering a quarter million.[40]

In spite of the modest annual precipitation totals, Sakha has abundant surface waters. The 7,000 or more rivers and tributary streams have a combined length of 1.5 million kilometers (932,000 miles). Largest among these is the magnificent Lena, whose 4,400-kilometer (2,732-mile) length ranks it among the ten greatest rivers of the world. Its tributary, the Vilyui River, itself over 2,650 kilometers (1,650 miles) long, drains the greater part of the central lowlands and much of the Central Siberian Plateau, including the Djarkhan area, while another tributary, the Aldan, gathers the waters of the southern plateau. The rivers of the northeast—the Yana, Indigirka, and Kolyma—flow down from the mountain ranges. All of Sakha's rivers drain to the Arctic, with the result that the mouths thaw later and freeze earlier than the headwaters, causing flooding over wide areas. The thaw on the lower Lena comes as late as mid-June, and the mouth usually freezes around the first of October. Sakha-Yakutia also has over 7,000 natural lakes, many trapped in round, saucer-shaped depressions.[41] Djarkhan village sits between two such lakes. The streams and lakes of Sakha yield a harvest of fish, as does the polar sea, both at a subsistence and commercial level.

## ECONOMY

At first glance, it seems improbable that a million inhabitants could wrest a living from so harsh and demanding an environment, but they do. In fact, until the economic crisis of 1998, Sakha was faring rather well. In spite of a 25 percent decline in industrial production between 1990 and 1995, the republic had a very low unemployment rate at mid-decade and far higher than average wages (and prices). All of this economic stability is now endangered by the recent crisis. In the autumn of 1998, the republic's government declared a state of emergency because inadequate winter provisions and fuel had arrived via the Arctic Ocean route, due largely to Russia's fiscal insolvency.[42]

In the total workforce at the most recent census in Sakha, 14 percent worked in mining, 4 percent in manufacturing, 11 percent in construction, 13 percent in agriculture, 1 percent in forestry, and 53 percent in the service sector, including transportation. As recently as 1993, 89 percent of the workforce was employed in government-owned enterprises, though that proportion has since fallen significantly. By 1998 the unemployment rate had risen to 13.6 percent.[43]

Mining remains the key to the modern economy of Sakha. The republic has all the elements listed on the periodic table buried in its landscape. Local legend says that when an ancient god of creation flew over Sakha, holding in his hands all the riches of the earth, his fingers went numb from the cold and he dropped everything. Known mineral reserves in Sakha are worth an estimated ten trillion dollars today. Because of that legendary wealth, during the Soviet period the republic served as a raw material appendage of the centralized economy, and the extractive processes led to the creation of industrial cities and towns.[44] Mining accounts for 75 percent of Sakha's gross domestic product, and 85 percent of the republic's revenues come from diamonds, followed in importance by gold, antimony, uranium, tin, coal, and natural gas. The republic provides 98 percent of Russia's diamonds, 21 percent of its gold, and all of the antimony. More than thirty oil and gas fields are found in Sakha. Newly acquired economic autonomy led to close cooperation with the DeBeers international diamond cartel. About 60 percent of Russia's foreign exchange at present is derived from Siberian resources, and the Sakha Republic contributes mightily to this enterprise.[45] Djarkhan village plays no role in this extractive industrial economy.

The mining industry suffers not only from the economic crisis in Russia, but also from the republic's remoteness and poorly developed land transport system (Map 1.2). The most common routes, as in czarist times, remain the rivers, especially when they are frozen. Rail transport ranks second in freight tonnage. A spur of the Baikal-Amur railroad of Russia's Trans-Siberian system has been built into the mining districts of the Aldan Plateau in the south. Sakha has 25,000 kilometers (15,500 miles) of drivable roads, only 11 percent of which are paved and 20 percent graveled. Main federal highways link the capital Yakutsk to Magadan on the Pacific Coast and the Amur region to the south, though these lack river bridges. Fully half of the road system can be used only in winter, when the surface is frozen, and then with difficulty. The shortcomings of the road and rail systems prompted the development of abundant airline connections, even to small places. In spite of these difficulties, Sakha participates in foreign trade. Japan is the principal partner, receiving 25 percent of all exports and sending 36 percent of the imports.[46]

These modern economic enterprises stand in marked contrast to traditional livelihoods, such as those pursued at Djarkhan village. Before the Communist revolution, the scattered inhabitants of Sakha-Yakutia made their living mainly by breeding livestock, raising a few subsistence crops, hunting, fishing, and gathering. At the close of the nineteenth century, over 98 percent of the Sakhalar lived in rural settlements. Despite the harsh climate, crop agriculture is possible in some regions. A growing season of only 80 to 130 days characterizes the central and southwestern sections of the republic. Agriculture increased in the Soviet period, and though Sakha lies on the very outermost margins of crop raising, grains can be cultivated in some places. The principal agricultural products are beef and dairy cattle, reindeer, Yakut horses, and poultry. Most of the agricultural land has been privatized at the cooperative level in recent years, a movement that also touched Djarkhan.[47]

## PARALLEL WORLDS

The jarring geographical juxtaposition of traditional and modern economies, of rural and urban, creates what we might best call "parallel worlds" in Sakha. These wildly contrasted ways of life exhibit fundamental differences in livelihood, worldview, standards of living, cultural landscape, food, clothing, and housing—the total lifestyle.

One of these parallel worlds is found in the capital city of Yakutsk, which, though founded in 1632, belongs in every sense to the modern age. The city is the administrative, commercial, cultural, and educational center of the republic and, possessing nearly a quarter of Sakha's population, its dominance is unchallenged. The foreign visitor will reach Yakutsk by flying into the international airport, a hub that has direct flight connections not only to many other Siberian cities, but also to Moscow, only six hours distant, and to foreign lands such as Greece, China, Turkey, and the United Arab Emirates. The visitor will likely travel via the republic's airline, fittingly called Diamonds of Sakha. Once arrived, the visitor will learn that in Yakutsk one can study diverse languages, including French, Japanese, Mongolian, English, German, and Chinese in both secondary schools and colleges. He or she can buy fine furs or diamond jewelry produced at local factories and attend opera or ballet performances. One also finds the Academy of Sciences of Sakha, three universities, the Pushkin Public Library with more than one million books, unique research organizations such as the Permafrost Studies Institute, and the Institute of Cosmic Studies. People dress as elegantly as those in Paris and London, and Japanese automobiles fill the streets, so many in fact that traffic jams are an almost daily occurrence. To be sure, much of this "culture" represents rapid change—another trait that does not fit the mythic image of Siberia—for in Soviet times no one would have dreamed that most people would have cars of their own or that the streets of Yakutsk would become hazardous.[48]

The bustling capital city represents only one unique reality, one of the parallel worlds in Sakha. If you fly a few hours northeast, some 870 kilometers, from Yakutsk to the coldest place in the world—the Oimyakon Plateau—you come to a very different, second parallel world, the gold-mining town of Ust'-Nera, situated in a broad, high valley, guarded by the jagged peaks and ridges of the Cherskiy Mountains (Maps 1.2, 1.5). This raw settlement, at north latitude 64°34', was founded as a forced labor camp, or gulag, in 1950, a status it retained for the following six years. Ust'-Nera is representative of dozens of similar places devoted to extractive industry in Sakha, and is populated almost exclusively by Russians. Life centers on the mine. A web of raised, insulated pipes carrying byproduct heat from the coal-fired power plant crisscrosses the town. These pipes, elevated to prevent them from thawing the permafrost, allow Ust'-Nerans to survive the bitterest cold in relative comfort. The town has experienced an all-time record low temperature of −72°C (−97°F).[49] One will not find much cultural life, for Ust'-Nera is all about work, production, and wages. Most of the inhabitants are relative newcomers, who arrived in Sakha to make money and then go back to European Russia. But some, captured by the romance of life on the very edge of the civilized world, stayed for good. The planners of Ust'-Nera did not provide the local workers with attractive housing or noteworthy cultural and educational institutions. The inhabitants once received two to three times the wages as their counterparts back in European Russia and therefore were expected to endure hardships. Even so, the residents often display a touching fondness and attachment to their small town, though they are aware it is a far from perfect place to live. In Sakha, people have the ability to establish homes under quite difficult conditions.

To go from Yakutsk or Ust'-Nera to a third parallel world—that of the traditional reindeer herders on the treeless tundra of northern Sakha—is to move in both space and time, so great are the contrasts. Conditions in this Arctic region are also very severe. The winter is long and windy, and summer lasts only a few weeks. The Evenks, Evens, Chukchis, and Yukagirs who live in this area prefer cold temperatures, because the abundant surface waters, when thawed, serve as a breeding ground for mosquitoes and also hinder movement across the land. Such movement is essential, because the herders are migratory and often shift the location of their camps. They live in tents and have a minimal material culture, but all of their clothing, tools, and implements are suited for the environment. Through thousands of years these people learned how to make their living in this least hospitable habitat.[50]

A fourth parallel world exists in the agricultural villages of the Central Yakut Plain. The great majority of these places are dominantly Sakhan in population, and such villages serve as the stronghold of traditional Yakut culture. Djarkhan, our village, is one of them, and in chapter 2 we turn our attention to this remarkable place.[51]

# 2 · THE SNOW-MUFFLED VILLAGE

Djarkhan, Bella Jordan's birthplace and ancestral home, lies deep in the "snow-muffled forests" of southwestern Sakha, where the solitude of the boreal woodlands is broken only at wide intervals by such isolated farming villages (Maps 1.2 and 2.1).[1] In this remote settlement, she was born in the dark depths of December, near the time of the winter solstice, in the year 1961. Her mother, Olga Danilovna Tikhonova, had returned to Djarkhan shortly before her birth so that Bella could be born in her village. At that time Olga worked as a dentist in the town of Suntar, the county seat, 86 kilometers (53 miles) distant by road. Motherless from the age of six, Olga became the pride of Djarkhan when she went away and earned a degree from the Irkutsk Medical Institute. Her sudden and unannounced return to the village only two weeks before Bella's birth surprised friends and relatives. They could not understand why she would abandon the modern medical facilities in Suntar, perhaps risking her life, to deliver a baby in the remote village. Years later, when asked to explain her decision, Olga replied evasively, but we think we know the reason. The Sakhalar are sensitive about the precise locale of birth, about community, family, and attachment to place. Healing and restorative powers reside in one's native place, particularly if it is an ancestral village. Olga wanted Bella to be a part of a familiar and nurturing locale, one dear to her Yakut heart. Olga's wish came true, for spiritually Bella has never completely left the village and her visits have been frequent. That this book was written provides evidence of her mystical attachment to Djarkhan. Another, very perceptive Russian writer might have had Bella in mind when he wrote that "every one of us has a small corner of this vast motherland where we were born and to which we forever remain attached, in spirit if not in body."[2]

In that mood, we commence our place-portrait, telling of a people in a remote and exotic corner of the world wresting a living from a hard land over a span of three and a half centuries. Unfortunately, such village-level studies remain rare, not just for Siberia, but throughout Russia, which is a pity, because local studies provide the very stuff of geography in its purest, most basic form.[3]

Though it evokes strong emotions among its natives, Djarkhan objectively viewed is in most all respects a typical Yakut farm village. It represents many similar places, and the majority of ethnic Sakhalar still live in settlements like Djarkhan. In 1970, fewer than one in five among them resided in cities and towns, and today the proportion is still only about one in four.[4] The countryside of the Sakha Republic has remained firmly Yakut in culture throughout the long period of Russian rule. We must go to places such as Djarkhan to understand the parallel world of Yakut rural culture.

## SITUATION AND REMOTENESS

Toward its middle reaches, the Vilyui River, the major left-bank tributary of the great Lena, traverses a large southward loop or bend in the western reaches of the Central Yakut Plain (Map 2.2).[5] Djarkhan village, also known by its older, traditional name of Arylakh, is nestled within that wide riverine arc, deep inside the broad interfluve, tucked away from the Vilyui. The village belongs to the expansive county, or *ulus,* of Suntar, named for

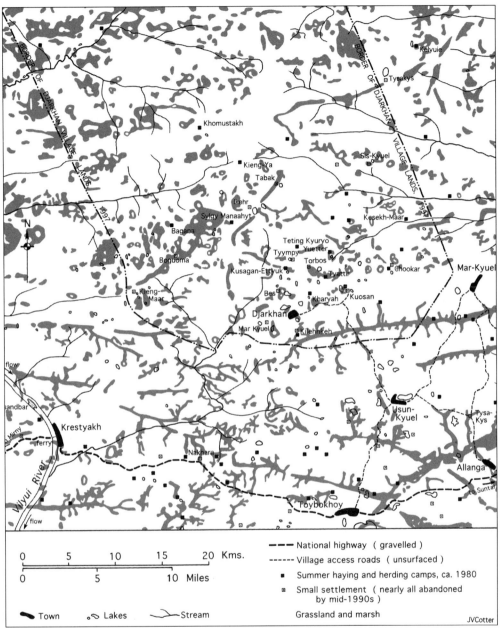

Map 2.1. *Djarkhan and surrounding parts of the Vilyui Bend region. Grassy alases and streamside meadows abound in the area, explaining the concentration of villages, hamlets, haying camps, and herding camps.* (Sources: *Manuscript maps in the village council hall, Djarkhan;* "*SSSR/RSFSR/Yakutskaya ASSR*" *1980–82; Atlas Sel'skogo 1989, 48.*)

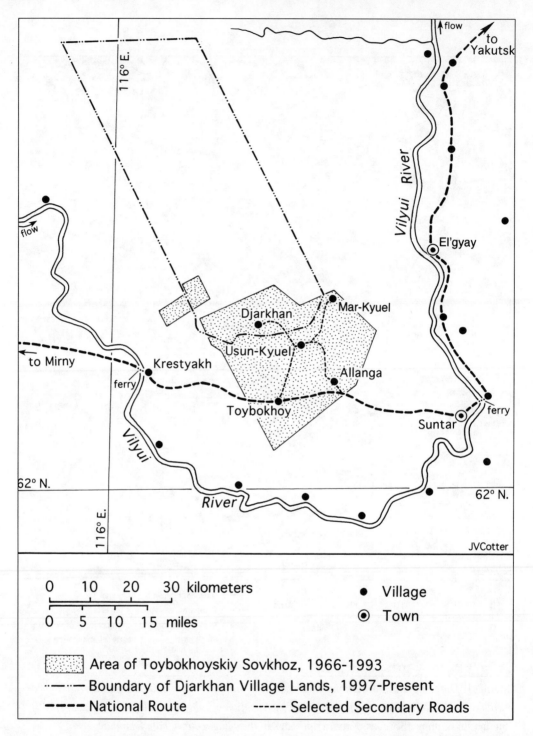

Map 2.2. *Vilyui Bend region, showing basic locations and the borders of the late-Soviet state farm and the post-Soviet borders of Djarkhan village lands. Because of deterioration, the dirt track from Usun-Kyuel to Allanga is no longer used by trucks or cars. Even the national route between Suntar and Mirny became temporarily impassable during flooding in the summer of 1998. (Sources: Atlas Sel'skogo 1989, 48, 54; manuscript map mounted on the wall of the office of the Suntar ulus governor, in Suntar town; manuscript maps in the Djarkhan village council hall; field observations.)*

the town of about nine thousand inhabitants, which serves as its seat. Suntar *ulus* is very sparsely settled and has over two square kilometers for each inhabitant (1.17 persons per square mile).[6]

More precisely, Djarkhan lies at 62°21' north latitude, a scant 470 kilometers (292 miles) south of the Arctic Circle and well within the "polar lands," as defined in the journal *Polar Geography.* Given the length and severity of the Siberian winter, it seems improbable that a farming settlement could exist at so high a latitude. Djarkhan stands in a flat lowland plain at an elevation of 215 meters (705 feet) above sea level, flanked at a distance in three directions by expansive plateaus.[7]

The village is by any definition remote, situated at the end of a poorly maintained dirt track. To reach the outside world, one must follow that seasonably impassible track for 31 kilometers (19 miles), passing the neighboring village of Usun-Kyuel ("Long lake") to reach Toybokhoy, on the graveled national highway linking Suntar town to the diamond-mining city of Mirny (Maps 2.1, 2.2). Upon reaching the national route at Toybokhoy, one must travel an additional 55 kilometers (34 miles) east to Suntar or, crossing several venerable ferries, 179 kilometers (111 miles) west to Mirny. Even the graveled national route becomes impassible for automobiles at times, as happened in the summer of 1998 due to flooding. In order to attend a funeral in Mirny, some Djarkhan kinfolks had to ride on a tractor for three days along the muddy national highway. First-class airmail letters take six weeks between the United States and the village.

At 116°41' east longitude, Djarkhan lies fully 13° west of the republic's capital, Yakutsk, requiring a journey of 1,072 kilometers (666 mi.) over a largely unpaved, route with no bridges, stretches of which are passable only in winter. Small wonder that co-author Terry, in 1997, was the first American and only the sixth foreigner ever to set foot in Djarkhan. Fellow Texan geographer Victor Mote, in 1985, became the first foreigner ever to visit the rural Vilyui Bend country, but he only got as far as Toybokhoy.[8]

Even the *ulus* seat, Suntar, is isolated. While the town lies on the banks of the navigable Vilyui River, no regular or reliable passenger boat connections extend beyond other, downstream river ports, such as Nyurba, though it is usually possible, with great patience and perseverance, to reach Yakutsk by such boats. No bus connections to the capital exist. Airline travel, very expensive by any standards, links Suntar's dirt landing strip to Yakutsk and a few other places in the Republic. In effect, one must choose between a tortuous, little-traveled seasonal road, an outrageously expensive airline, or a tiresome and unreliable riverboat to reach the outside world. These three transport modes all foster isolation for the *ulus* and village.

Djarkhan's isolation is somewhat mitigated by the presence of several other sizable villages in the vicinity. Usun-Kyuel lies about 13 kilometers (8 miles) to the southeast—somewhat farther by road, Mar-Kyuel 20 kilometers (12.5 miles) east, and the previously mentioned Toybokhoy, a larger agro-town, to the south. Other nearby villages and hamlets, such as Kuosan ("Down in the hollow"), only 7 kilometers (4 miles) to the northeast, have all been abandoned in the past half-century (Map 2.1).

In spite of this isolation, the people of Djarkhan are not the unsophisticated, provincial peasants one might expect. If the world has not come to them, they somehow managed to go to it. In Soviet times, student groups and village leaders went to Moscow and Leningrad on occasion, and among the men are veterans of Soviet operations in Vietnam and Cuba, among other places. A few villagers have visited Alaska. They did not stand and stare even at the first visitor from America.

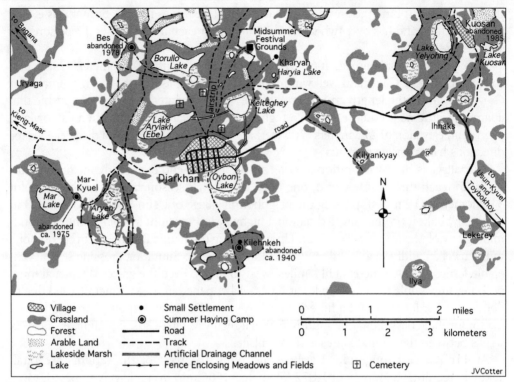

Map 2.3. *Vicinity of Djarkhan, showing vegetation, waters, and other features. All outlying settlements are largely or completely abandoned.* (Sources: *Manuscript maps in the land-use planning ministry of Suntar ulus, Suntar town; field observations.*)

The people of Djarkhan welcome visitors, showering them with gracious hospitality, food, and gifts. Though not wealthy—far from it—they freely and generously give away possessions and even cash. When Bella visited the village in 1996, as a university graduate student, the people of Djarkhan assumed she needed money and pressed some five hundred dollars into her hand. Partly, too, this generous gift reflected their deep veneration of education. When Bella and Terry returned to the village in 1997 as newlyweds, an array of fine gifts was offered, including hunting knives, *kumyss* vessels, birchbark containers, and jewelry, as well as cash. A second wedding celebration took place, with many villagers in attendance.

## A SENSE OF PLACE

Djarkhan consists of a loose cluster of log houses scattered somewhat haphazardly through an imperfect gridiron of wide dirt streets, positioned alongside the shallow, pretty lake called Oybon, one of those "little villages nestled near water" so common in the Central Yakut Plain (Map 2.3).[9] At the beginning of the twenty-first century, the village has 639 inhabitants, of whom over 53 percent are males—a departure from the Russian

Figure 2.1. *The Yakutian language prevails in Djarkhan. The large sign above the door reads* WELCOME TO LEARNING, *and teacher Zinaida Popova stands in front of a smaller sign that identifies the Djarkhan Upper School. (Photograph by Bella Bychkova Jordan, 1996.)*

norm, for women far outnumber men in the country's population. All but three of the villagers are ethnic Sakhalar, the tiny minority consisting of an Even, a Dolgan, and a Russian. In 1995, Djarkhan's only Kazak died and the sole Belarussian moved away.[10] The village's ethnic purity is extreme. In rural Sakha as a whole, Yakuts form just three-quarters of the population.[11]

The Yakutian language prevails in the streets, shops, schools, and homes of the village (Fig. 2.1). In this respect, Djarkhan reflects linguistically the total Yakut population of Sakha, among whom only 3 percent listed Russian as their first language in 1994. Most residents are not bilingual; many possess little ability to understand or speak Russian. It almost seems as if the Russians had never come to the place.[12]

Djarkhan has about 196 families, each living in their own private residence. Marriage is clearly a popular institution; only 13 unmarried women over 25 years of age and 19 single men over 30 live in Djarkhan. Widowers typically remarry. As soon as a couple marries, they build a house, often on the same lot with the parental home (Fig. 2.2). Ten or more young families were constructing houses when we visited, promising future demographic vitality to Djarkhan. Twelve more were erected in 1998. Until very recently, the number of births far exceeded deaths, as in 1993, when twenty-one children were born and only three persons died. As you walk in the streets, children are seen at every hand (Figs. 2.3 and 2.4). The natural population decline now typical of Russia does not yet characterize Djarkhan, and robust rural population growth typified all of the Sakha Republic, from the late 1940s to the middle 1980s. In 1998 in the village, six births

Figure 2.2. *Two log houses in Djarkhan, standing on the same lot. On the right is the parental home; on the left stands the new house of one of their recently married children. Note the stack of firewood. (Photograph by Bella Bychkova Jordan, 1996.)*

Figure 2.3. *Village children gathered at the entrance to a log house. (Photograph by Bella Bychkova Jordan, 1996.)*

*Figure 2.4. Djarkhan has no shortage of youngsters. Note the fir trees in the background. (Photograph by Bella Bychkova Jordan, 1996.)*

precisely balanced the six reported deaths. Beginning in 1995 the total rural population of Sakha started to decline, due mainly to mounting net emigration. The signs of the process can be seen in Djarkhan as well. In 1996 several newly built cottages stood abandoned by young couples who had departed for Suntar, Mirny, and even Yakutsk in search of jobs. The underrepresentation of females in the village's population is the result of the greater tendency of young, unmarried women to emigrate.[13]

Wandering the dirt streets of Djarkhan in the summertime, one sees a loose assemblage of small wooden houses and outbuildings (Fig. 2.5); an abundance of haystacks and firewood piles for the long winter, never far ahead (Fig. 2.6); lush green potato patches thriving in the long hours of sunlight; picket fences lining the streets and enclosing the gardens (Fig. 2.7); cows lying in the streets or wandering home from the pastures to be milked, and the countless fresh patties of manure they drop along the way (Fig. 2.8); well-fed, long-haired Siberian hunting dogs lying about panting (124 of them to be exact, according to the meticulously taken annual village census); a few of the community's 62 cats (who have achieved a recent population explosion, doubling in number in five years); numerous children on bicycles; a thin scattering of trees; and every now and then, an automobile, jeep, motorcycle, or tractor, stirring up dust or splashing mud (Figs. 2.9 and 2.10). Do not expect running water or indoor plumbing in Djarkhan. Cold temperatures and the permanently frozen subsurface make these impossible. Water is hauled from the lake, or else gathered in rain barrels at the eaves. It is stored as ice blocks in cellars during the winter. A privy stands behind each house, built over a pit dug down to the ice level, though a few affluent residents have installed indoor chemical toilets. Imagine the trek to these privies in temperatures of −40°. Imagine, too, the thaw of late spring, when, as

Figure 2.5. *Typical Djarkhan street scene, with cattle, firewood, log houses, farm wagon, and barn. Note the electricity wires. (Photograph by Bella Bychkova Jordan, 1996.)*

Figure 2.6. *Hay for the long winter—the only source of feed for cattle during an eight-month period. Note the traditional rail fence. (Photograph by Bella Bychkova Jordan, 1996.)*

Figure 2.7. *A fenced vegetable garden beside a potato patch and haystack in Djarkhan. (Photograph by Bella Bychkova Jordan, 1996.)*

Figure 2.8. *Cows resting in the muddy streets of Djarkhan. In the background is the World War II memorial and the village council hall. (Photograph by Terry G. Jordan-Bychkov, 1997.)*

Figure 2.9. *Teenagers cruising the dirt streets of Djarkhan on a motorbike with wheeled sidecar, the most common motor vehicle in the village. (Photograph by Terry G. Jordan-Bychkov, 1997.)*

Figure 2.10. *One of Djarkhan's four surviving functional tractors roars down the village's main east-west street. (Photograph by Terry G. Jordan-Bychkov, 1997.)*

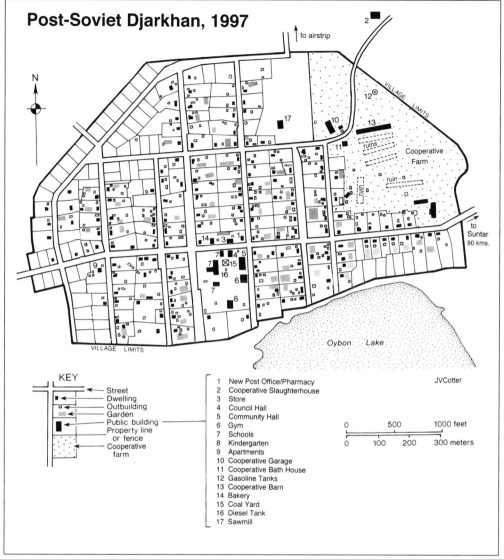

Map 2.4. *Post-Soviet Djarkhan, 1997. Compare this village map to map 4.1, late-Soviet Djarkhan.* (Sources: *Manuscript map in the village council hall, Djarkhan; field observations.*)

visitor Victor Mote said, "a winter's worth of frozen feces and urine" suddenly becomes biodegradable.

The visitor wandering through Djarkhan will sooner or later come across the administrative and institutional center, a loose cluster of modest public buildings made of wood. These include several schools, providing education through high school; the village council hall; a new post office/pharmacy; a sports complex; a recreation hall, containing a library, theater, and dance floor; and a store selling groceries, clothing, and other necessities (Map 2.4).

Visitors will look in vain for a church. None have ever stood in Djarkhan or for that matter in any other rural settlements of the Vilyui Bend, even in czarist times. In Sakha as a whole today, only 30 percent of all ethnic Yakuts describe themselves as religious "believers," and these adhere to traditional shamanism, mixed only lightly with Russian Orthodoxy.[14] So far, the Djarkhan villagers have been spared the attention of evangelical missionaries from the West, though their arrival is perhaps only a matter of time.

Such a pedestrian description of the village misses the most essential geographical attribute of the place. The people of Djarkhan, including those who now reside elsewhere, share Bella's strong loyalty and emotional bond to the village. They are deeply attached to it, in a way mobile Americans can scarcely imagine. Djarkhan reunions are held at midsummer's festivals in Yakutsk and Suntar. At such gatherings and in celebrations in Djarkhan, the participants enthusiastically sing the village song. Nearby Toybokhoy also has its song, so melodic that it is known and sung all over the republic. The lyrics to "Noble Djarkhan," composed by Zinaida Popova and translated from the Yakutian, are as follows:

(Verse)
Our old men, who tease and tell tales,
our old women, such gracious hosts,
our young women, so very beautiful,
our sons-in-law, strong and vigorous.

(Refrain)
Our village possesses much that is good,
like other places,
its people so hospitable and kind,
as in other places.
My native village and land,
Noble Djarkhan!

(Verse)
Our gentle daughters-in-law,
our brave young men,
our youths who sing so beautifully,
our skilled and talented folk.

(Repeat Refrain)

(Verse)
Our children who love
to run and play,
our youths who delight
to dance and wrestle.

(Repeat Refrain)

Besides song—and the Sakhalar love dearly to sing—few sounds disrupt the peace and quiet of Djarkhan, as if the villagers seek to emulate the silence of the surrounding prairie and forest and to avoid angering ancient spirits. Even the village teenagers, gathered in front of the council hall and school on a summer's eve seem uninterested in making noise. In the absence of sound, color can dominate the senses. In the brief summer, on a sunny day, and many such occur, the eye is filled with greens—the forest, the prairie, the gardens —and blues—the sky and the lake. These cool hues are repeated symbolically in the horizontal bars of the republic's beautiful flag, flying above the village council hall. Mother Russia's red-blue-white tricolor banner is nowhere to be seen. Red, the color of revolution and Communism, has been largely expunged from Djarkhan's landscape, appearing now only in the colors of the sunset. In winter, the greens and blues give way to a blanket of white, covering land and water alike, and sounds become even more muffled. The snow tries to conceal the faint, feeble marks and noises of humankind, restoring the peace and harmony of the Yakutian wilderness.

## WINTER

Yakutia, as described earlier, is notorious for the severity of its winters. Djarkhan enjoys a somewhat milder winter than most other parts of the republic. In the arcane classification employed by Russian climatologists, the Vilyui Bend belongs in "the first agroclimate region of the first thermal zone," and we can equate the doubled "first" to relative warmth. Others describe the local climate as "dry microthermal." But make no mistake; the winters at Djarkhan are frigid. In fact, the average annual temperature is below freezing. The lowest temperature ever recorded in the Vilyui Bend was −58°C (−72°F), warmer to be sure than Yakutsk's record of −63°C (−81°F), but still extreme by world standards.[15]

Winters are not merely severe, but also long. The first frosts at Djarkhan usually come during the early weeks of September, and by the middle of October the ground is covered with snow. But the Sakhalar do not consider October a winter month and instead begin the season around November 20, when days become shorter and darker. A century ago, a visiting scholar who had spent years in the Yakutian countryside described how "the shadow of the winter night grows and the darkness becomes ever thicker."[16] While only about one-eighth of the annual precipitation at Djarkhan falls in winter, snowfalls are frequent during the comparatively warmer months when the cold season is establishing its grip (Figs. 2.11 and 2.12). This is a time of "eternal snowstorms and repulsive slush."[17]

Next comes the bitter cold, which prevails for about three months. Temperatures remain extremely low, and even the difference between day and night readings is not great, since daylight scarcely exists. Snowfall gives way to fogs and ice dusts. A white, heavy fog forms, hanging close to the ground, especially in and near the village. Called "habitation fog," it consists of frozen condensation from heated buildings, farm animals, and people. The thick, bitterly cold air holds the frost fog close to the ground and does not allow it to rise.[18]

Ice dust, another phenomenon of the depths of winter, consists of tiny sharp particles of ice floating in the air. If you do not cover your face with a scarf, the ice dust stings like a thousand needles. When the temperature falls below −55°C (−67°F), as it occasionally does in Djarkhan, one hears a sound the Sakhalar poetically call the "whispering of the stars," a curious rustling or tinkling sound made as your exhalation instantly freezes.[19] When snowflakes begin falling again, it means that temperatures are warming and winter is waning.

Figure 2.11. *The snow-muffled village on a winter's day. (Photograph by Aleksandra Tikhonova, 1997.)*

On the whole, winter in the village is the white kingdom of quietness. Everything—the ground, snow-muffled trees, and lakes—sleeps deeply frozen. Even the sky has a peculiar look, as if it were made of opaque glass. The sun is a fleeting visitor. After a few hours hovering low in the south, it hurries back below the horizon. Clouds obscure it much of the time, depriving the villagers of even this fleeting sight, but on a fair day the weak winter sun can do miracles. Its rays reflect off millions of particles in the packed snow in all the colors of the rainbow. The whole white landscape glitters as if it were covered with diamond dust. The depressing darkness of the winter is interrupted sometimes by a magic salutation from Mother Nature—the Northern Lights. They hang in the transparent black sky like huge curtains woven of golden and silver threads. Another very peculiar phenomenon associated with wintertime is that noises can be heard at the distance of 3 to 5 kilometers (2 or 3 miles), a result of high atmospheric pressure, which enhances the speed of sound.

The villagers claim that winters have become somewhat less severe in recent times, during their lifespan. Some climatological and cryological research supports this claim, pointing to the subsidence of the permafrost layer. Other climatologists offer contradictory evidence, reporting that the Lena River basin was the only part of Russia where climatic severity actually increased in the 1980s. Ground temperatures rose between 1986 and 1991, only to decrease slightly in the next half-decade.[20] In any case, the winter remains very severe, and we should not imagine that the villagers of Djarkhan enjoy this season. One local woman said, "We endure winter, but we don't like it; toward the end of winter, your body feels tired, maybe because of some dietary deficiency."[21] The Sakhalar, trying to cope mentally with winter, long ago created vivid allegorical images of cold and freezes. In one, the winter cold is compared to a bull with two horns, one of which is broken on the fifth of March, the other on the twenty-fourth of April. After the fourteenth of May his whole body falls away.[22] Indeed, the white bull of winter resists the influence of the spring sun for a long time. In the modern age, coping with winter takes other, often bizarre forms. One villager videotapes her vegetable garden in the summer, for winter viewing.

Figure 2.12. *The perimeter of the Lake Oybon* alas, *bordering the fir trees, in the depth of winter. (Photograph by Aleksandra Tikhonova, 1997.)*

## SPRING, SUMMER, AND AUTUMN

In Djarkhan snowmelt begins April 17, on the average, and is usually completed by May 11. April in the Yakut calendar, *moos ustar,* means "The month when the ice breaks," but the name is misleading and derives from an ancient time, when the Sakhalar lived far to the south, in the semiarid steppes of Eurasia. The melting of snow usually ends ten days to a fortnight ahead of the icebreaking process in the rivers and lakes. The lakes near Djarkhan are fully free from ice only by the first days of June in a typical year, and the last frost comes around June 15.[23]

Djarkhan's spring passes swiftly, often lasting only part of May. It commences with strong winds, presenting a contrast to the long, almost windless winter. In the Vilyui region, the spring winds, blowing from either the north or southwest, quickly destroy the already weakened winter regime. They do not bring much precipitation, differentiating the Vilyui Valley from the rest of Yakutia. The villagers of Djarkhan begin sending their cattle out to pasture about the third week of May, beginning a four-month grazing period that defines the summer.

Others would say that summer begins with haying, the most important activity for the villagers, since they need to gather enough fodder to carry their animals through the eight cold months in the stalls. Haying usually begins just after the Yakut midsummer's celebration, at the solstice, which marks the Yakut New Year. In addition, the villagers must, during a short frost-free period that varies from fifty to seventy-five days, grow garden crops such as potatoes, cabbage, carrots, and radishes. Summer in the Vilyui Bend country usually begins warm and fair, and the vegetables grow rapidly in the almost continuous daylight.[24] The same sun that hid from view during long winter months hardly goes away at all during the so-called white nights, from the second half of May until mid-July. On Midsummer's Day, the sun remains above the horizon for nineteen hours, forty-five minutes at Djarkhan. The celebration lasts for two, sometimes three days, with various activities and competitions uninterrupted by darkness.[25]

Though the amounts of precipitation are modest, summer is the rainy season at Djarkhan. Of some 300 millimeters (12 inches) of annual precipitation, about half falls in summer, and sometimes as much as 200 millimeters (8 inches). The true rainy season occurs in the last half of summer, after mid-July, though dry interludes usually occur even then. If too much rain falls, or too frequently, haymaking is endangered, as in 1997, when the far greater part of the crop was ruined, creating a dire emergency. If too little rain falls, the Vilyui dwindles to a stream too small to navigate, as happened in the summer of 1990.[26]

The summer brings other unpleasantries. June is the time of mosquitoes, July is the realm of biting flies, and August belongs to the midges. Clouds of such insects can descend on an unsuspecting person. Heat, too, can become oppressive. Temperatures in Djarkhan rise as high as 35° to 38°C (95° to 100°F). Such heat, if combined with several weeks of drought, can bring forest fires, as happened near the end of July in 1996. Smoke filled the air and hung over the land like a warm habitation fog, irritating the eyes and throat. These conditions lasted for about two weeks, because once a fire starts in the dense depth of the *taiga,* it is almost impossible to extinguish. We could not see the beautiful blue sky or enjoy the sudden absence of insects. Traditionally, Yakuts did not even try to put out these fires, because they encourage the growth of grasses. In fact, they often deliberately fire the *alas* meadows after the last hay mowing, in late August, when the remaining grasses have been deadened by frost. Travelers in Sakha have reported smoky conditions in August for centuries.[27]

The Sakhalar say summer ends on Saint Nicholas Day—August 20—and mothers do not allow their children to swim in the lakes after that, no matter how warm the temperature. The first frost comes around August 15, on the average. As September arrives, the temperatures decrease rapidly, as does precipitation. Light rain occasionally mingles with snow. Still, during September the average temperatures remain above freezing. During the autumnal day the temperature can rise as high as 20°C (68°F), and at night it can drop to −11° or −12°C (8° to 10°F). The permanent snow cover forms in October, and during this time the greater part of winter precipitation falls. Nearby, the river, "Father Vilyui," begins to freeze and "the ice queen ascends her throne," as the local people say. In truth, "the country has no true fall," or "September comprises autumn." Instead, "the gigantic winter swallows the adjacent seasons," fall and spring alike.[28]

## LAND AND WATERS

The land within the Vilyui Bend, where Djarkhan stands, is an almost featureless flat plain, extending to the river in three directions and to a distant plateau escarpment on the north. Sluggish streams struggle to escape the plain, and a considerable part of the interfluve is in fact an area of internal drainage that does not reach the Vilyui, a phenomenon that owes as much to scant precipitation as to terrain. Only the subtlest landform features break the monotony of the plain—a myriad of saucer-shaped, shallow depressions, easily spotted on a map by the small oval lakes that occupy their center and which gather the waters that do not reach the river (Map 2.1).

The shallow depressions are called, in the Yakutian language, *alases,* a word now accepted in the scientific jargon of periglacial research.[29] To the American eye, an *alas* resembles the playa lakes trapped in the closed sinks of the High Plains of Texas or Kansas, but in fact their origin and character are quite different. To understand their development—and we should, since *alases* are the very basis of Yakut settlement and livelihood—the phenomenon of permafrost must be explained.

In the Ice Age, the Central Yakut Plain was never covered by glaciers, mainly because precipitation was too meager to allow them to develop. Instead, the bitterest cold prevailed, far more severe than today, causing the earth to freeze to a depth of hundreds of meters. The subsurface remains frozen to the present day, since the climate remains too cold to thaw the depths. The perpetually frozen subsurface forms the permafrost layer. Each summer the surface of the land around Djarkhan thaws to a depth of about 25 to 40 centimeters (10 to 16 inches) in lakeside bogs, 150 centimeters (5 feet) in grassy areas and up to 225 centimeters (7.5 feet) in a few sandy places. In winter, the Ice Age returns as the frozen condition expands upward to the surface again, leaving only the lakebeds and an adjacent layer of bottom-water above freezing.[30]

*Alases* develop in places where the permafrost melts to a greater depth, as might happen after a forest fire or any other destruction of the woodland, opening the land surface to the warmth of the summer sun. In this thawed place, a sink or depression forms in the land when the moisture in the ground shrinks as it converts from ice to water. This process is called thermokarst by periglacialists, and it created all the *alases* of the Vilyui Bend.[31]

As the *alases* formed, another and very wonderful thing happened, one that underlies the very existence of the Sakha people. The boreal forest did not reclaim the depressions, but instead they became open grassland surrounding the central lakes. On maps and aerial photographs, these oval prairies reveal the location of *alases* (Figs. 2.12 and 2.13). Such a map or photograph will also tell you where the population is concentrated, because the more *alases* an area has, the more Yakuts live there.

The lush grasses of the *alases* yield hay for herds of cattle and provide pasture for both horses and cows (Fig. 2.14). Without the prairies, the Sakhalar, a herding people, could not have colonized the Vilyui Bend. In addition to *alases,* the Yakut pioneers found numerous streamside grasslands called *yuryakhs,* produced by seasonal overflows. These grassy wetlands stand out on the map as linear prairies (Map 2.1). Djarkhan occupies a particularly favored site, where several adjacent *alases* coalesced to form an extended contiguous prairie resembling a wooded steppe (Map 2.3). Moreover, other fine *alases* lie nearby, as do many *yuryakhs.* The Djarkhan village lands include 1,817 hectares (4,490 acres) of natural pasture and another 2,954 hectares (7,300 acres) of native meadow, a great abundance by comparison to most other villages.

The *alas* ecosystem consists of several concentric zones. Nearest to the lake, the innermost circle is boggy and covered with reeds and sedges. Odd little mounds called *thufurs,* created by the repeated freezing and thawing of water trapped in tiny depressions, dot the edge of the bog (Fig. 2.15). The second concentric belt has grasses mixed with wetland plants, and beyond it the true grassland begins, dominated by fescue, feathergrass, wild barley, sorrel, and koeleria. On the outer periphery of the *alases,* in the highest-lying and driest zone, grasses grow less lushly and are challenged by wormwood. The *yuryakh* ecosystem, by contrast, is more in the nature of a streamside wetland.[32]

Nor should we overlook the *alas* flowers, which lend another element of beauty. The first spring flower, an anemone called *nyurgusun,* is of special importance for the Sakhalar. It starts growing beneath the snow and opens its pink, pale-golden, and white cups as early

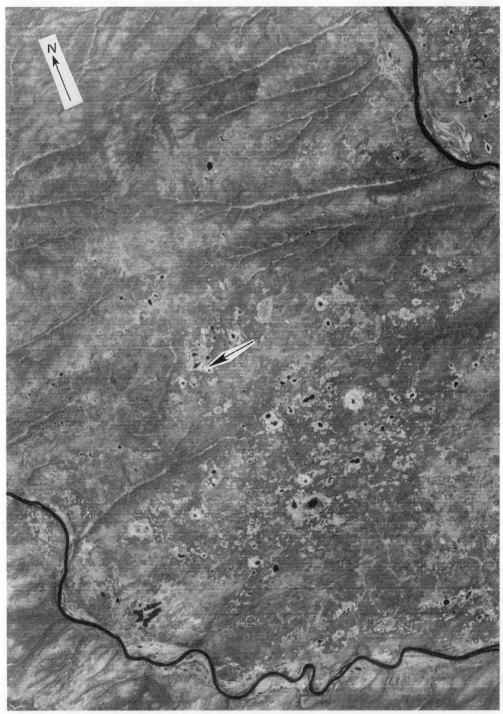

Figure 2.13. *Part of the Vilyui Bend country, as viewed on August 31, 1973, by the U.S. Landsat spy satellite. This remote image was recently declassified. The arrow indicates the location of Djarkhan. The alases, pale in tone, are clearly visible in the taiga, as are lakes, which appear black.*
(Source: *The collection of Landsat images housed at the University of California at Santa Barbara, film can 9E0541, header 42803, scene E-1404-03084, band 7, frame 190.*)

Figure 2.14. *Cutting hay in the Lake Borullo alas, north of Djarkhan. Most of this hay crop, one of the most abundant in many years, was lost during heavy rains. (Photograph by Terry G. Jordan-Bychkov, July 10, 1997.)*

as the first days of May. An abundance of these flowers promises the villagers a good hay harvest. Its beauty and vitality are another reason why Yakuts treat this flower differently from others. They give its name to boys and girls alike, and consider it a symbol of both the Yakut soul and faithful love. By June the *nyurgusun* has been replaced by many other flowers, including legions of dandelions.

Flowers lend part of the truly magical quality to the *alases,* a quality felt deeply by the Yakuts. When they sing of "the *alas* of my father," tears come to their eyes. The Sakhalar remain, in their heart of hearts, a Turkic people of the steppes, and when their ancestors discovered, so unexpectedly, these *alases* deep in the midst of the somber Siberian *taiga,* it must have seemed as if the gods were guiding and rewarding them. They have never forgotten that divine intercession and remain deeply attached to these beautiful grassy places, these little "steppe isles."[33]

Part of the emotional appeal of the *alases* and their beauty is provided by the pretty blue lakes nestled in the middle. They, too, are essential to Yakut life. While often somewhat mineralized, the lakes provide drinking water, contain fish, and supply irrigation for garden crops. Four sizable lakes flank the village of Djarkhan—Oybon ("Hole for fishing cut in ice"), beside whose very shore the village stands; Ebe ("Grandmother"), lying on the opposite side of Djarkhan and also called Arylakh ("Where *alases* interconnect and groves of forest exist"), the older, traditional name of both Ebe and Djarkhan; Kelteghey ("Crooked" or "Crescent-shaped," even though it is round!); and Borullo ("Place of the white-tailed eagle") (Fig. 2.15). The four lakes have a cumulative area of about 400 hectares (1,000 acres). Inflow to them is greatest during the spring thaw, but none of the lakes rises

Figure 2.15. *Lake Oybon and its* thufur-*infested perimeter. Olga Tikhanova and schoolteacher Zinaida Popova stand on the shaky board walkway over the bog used by villagers to fetch water in buckets from the lake. (Photograph by Bella Bychkova Jordan, 1996.)*

high enough to send waters to the Vilyui, though occasionally the edge of the village gets flooded.[34] Several additional, very small lakes lie near Djarkhan, but even they possess value and importance, as is suggested by the fact that the villagers long ago ascribed the spirits of oxen to them.[35]

## THE TAIGA

Expansive as the *alases* and *yuryakhs* are in the Vilyui Bend, the greater part of the land bears a forest cover. Flying in the small, propeller-driven airplane that provided a link from Djarkhan to Suntar, the passengers saw mainly a carpet of dark green below, the *taiga*. While the Sakhalar, as a herding people, prize grasslands more than forests, they also depend on the *taiga* for many of life's necessities. It gives them food, including many essential vitamins, as well as fur, firewood, and logs for their houses and barns.

While the deciduous needleleaf Dahurian larch is the dominant species in the Vilyui Bend as throughout the Yakutian *taiga,* the forest has a decidedly mixed character. Pines grow here, and the Sakhalar especially value them. Traditionally they ate processed pine sapwood instead of bread. According to the Evenks, "Where one finds pine, one finds Yakuts."[36] Pine is not dominant in the region, accounting for only one of every twenty trees, but Yakuts value it above all others. The toponymic element *Bes* refers to pines (Map 2.3). In contrast to the gloomy larch forest, the pine groves appear lighter, drier, more transparent and cleaner, lacking wind-fallen twigs and branches on the moss-covered forest floor. Birds and small animals abound in the pine forests. The Sakhalar love this type of woodland best and choose it for their traditional summer feasts.[37]

What differentiates Djarkhan vegetation from even the neighboring villages is the fir woods that surround it, acknowledged in place names such as *Kharyia, Kharyah,* and *Haryia* (Map 2.3).[38] The ragged tops of fir trees dominate the village skyline and become especially spectacular when reflected by the sunset in the lakes. The firs' beauty, shape, and evergreen character provide a symbol of Djarkhan. In 1988, after eight years of absence, Bella visited Djarkhan. All of her friends and relatives urged her to do so, because the aura of her birthplace, they said, lends strength and improves health. The Sakhalar believe in the power of places, and perhaps we should learn something from them. As Bella walked toward the village from the airstrip, she experienced the very vivid nostalgia that only a smell can arouse. She stopped and looked around, then saw a fallen fir branch that had wilted in the hot July sun. This heated fir resin suddenly evoked the whole world of her childhood that seemed to have floated away.

The white birch is another special, even sacred, tree for Yakuts, the place where the spirit of the land dwells. They love its slender, clean look, and the birch provides material for the traditional Yakut bowls and dishes famous for preserving milk products even in the absence of ice. The handles of hunting knives are also made of birch. The Sakhalar truly revere the pine and birch. Every now and then, in the depths of the forest your eyes will discern brightly colored spots on large trees of these species. Closer inspection reveals little ribbons of different hues that the people of Djarkhan have bound to the branches of an especially beautiful tree. When performing this ritual they make wishes or ask the spirits of the forest for protection and help.[39]

North of Djarkhan, where most of the village's lands lie, the forest changes. The firs disappear, replaced by a mixture of larches, pines, birches, and aspens, each seeking a particular type of soil, moisture level, and light exposure. The Dahurian larch requires a lot of sunlight and cannot survive in low, dark, and damp places. It usually flourishes on dry sandy or loamy soils. The pine also favors this type of soil and competes successfully for space with the larches.

The Vilyui Bend *taiga* hosts a diverse undergrowth of ash, willow, alder, and dwarf birch, and no fewer than sixty local varieties of lichens occur in the vicinity of Djarkhan. Berries grow in abundance and provide the main source of vitamin C in the villagers' diet. The women of the village dedicate at least several days, during short breaks in the hay-cutting season, when the grass needs to dry in the sun, to gathering berries. Most abundant is the red bilberry, followed by red and black currants, blueberries, and wild raspberries. Mushrooms grow in great variety near Djarkhan, but they are less popular with the Sakhalar, and before the Russians came, the natives did not consume mushrooms as food. Only powerful shamans knew how to use the few poisonous mushrooms for preparing hallucinogenic drinks for rituals. At the beginning of summer the forest floor is decorated with the white and pink blossoms of wild roses and buttercups, various berry bushes, and "march tea." Later, in midsummer the forest air fills with the sweetest fragrances, especially on a hot day when the scent of young larches spreads widely, and every flower opens it petals.[40]

The forest is also the scene of the hunt, yielding meat and furs. Djarkhan's hunting grounds lie northwest of the village, extending far into the wilderness that stretches in that direction, devoid of human settlements. Without the harvest of the hunt, without wood for fire and building or furs for clothing or berries and sapwood to diversify the diet, the Yakuts could not have survived in the Vilyui Bend. For all of these practical reasons, the Sakhalar came to revere the *taiga* almost as much as their beloved *alases*.

## SOILS

The *alases* are underlain by deep meadow *chernozems*—prairie black earth. Also referred to as *sapropel* soils, they have a 30- to 40-centimeter-thick (12- to 16-inch-thick) horizon of dark humus on top, granular in texture when dry and bearing polygonal permafrost-induced cracks. The meadow *chernozems* of the Vilyui Bend are also rich in phosphorus, and they thaw to a depth of 130 to 160 centimeters (45 to 63 inches) each summer, more than adequate to allow grain cultivation. Their only deficiency, in fact, is a mild salinity, a virtue for grazing and hay, since it provides needed salt for the herd animals. The salinity is not severe enough to prevent grain cultivation.

Discard, then, all stereotypes concerning sterile, acidic, leached, light-colored soils, or podsols, that supposedly characterize the *taiga* zone. Few expanses of podsols occur in the Vilyui Bend country. The permafrost blocks the downward leaching of nutrients necessary for severe podsolization. At the same time, the permafrost layer helps the soil retain adequate moisture to support plant growth, compensating for the modest precipitation amounts. The melting subsurface ice sends water upward, through capillary action. Even so, the thawed soils become very dry by the end of July, and the land "greedily absorbs" the rains of early August.[41]

Even the forested areas around Djarkhan lack true podsols, having instead weakly podsolized sandy loams that possess enough fertility to support meadow grasses or even grains if the forest cover were removed. About two-thirds of the lands belonging to Djarkhan village are underlain by such sandy loams. Extreme podsolization occurs only in patches of sandy soil, which thaw to a greater depth, but such soils occupy only 3 percent of the village lands. Peat bog soils underlie 5 percent of the land and are concentrated along the lakeshores.[42]

## A PASTORAL IDYLL

When the midsummer's festival has ended, a time of hard work awaits the villagers of Djarkhan. They disperse through the *alases* and *yuryakhs*, setting up camps even in distant places to cut and gather hay. The visitor is treated to a supremely pastoral view, a boreal Turkic extravaganza (Fig. 2.16). At every hand, near and far, villagers wielding scythes and hay rakes are hard at work, against the background of glittering blue lakes and the distant tree line. Dogs and children chase seagulls, who, in their search for food, abandon the lake waters and fly low over the meadows consuming grasshoppers stirred up by the hay cutters. Djarkhaners love to labor in the open air after the long, monotonous winter months of involuntarily confinement. This time of the year, when they can inhale the juices of freshly cut grass and enjoy the beauty of nature in all its splendor, compensates for the boredom and chill of the rural winter.

So idyllic a scene implies immutability, suggesting that Djarkhan has stood beside its lake for many centuries, from the time long ago when the Sakhalar first came to the Vilyui

Figure 2.16. *In the* alas *haymeadows of Djarkhan. (Photograph by Terry G. Jordan-Bychkov, 1997.)*

Bend. The same impression of continuity and timelessness is conveyed by the deep, emotional attachment of the villagers to Djarkhan and its role as a mystical place for them. Nevertheless, such an impression is false, for the village dates only from the 1930s and was a Soviet creation. True, Yakuts lived beside Oybon and Ebe long before Soviet surveyors laid out Djarkhan's streets, but those Sakhalar of old were neither villagers nor farmers. Chapter 3 examines life in the local *alases* before the time of the village.

# 3 · BEFORE A VILLAGE STOOD ON OYBON'S SHORE

The migratory path followed by Bella's ancestral Sakhalar to reach the Vilyui Bend and the shores of Lake Oybon, with its lush haymeadows, was both lengthy and unlikely. Yakuts belong to a pastoral culture of "deep antiquity" and originated in a faraway country. In ancient times, they lived among other Turkic nomadic tribes on the endless steppes of central Asia, far to the south of modern Sakha, near fabled Lake Baikal. Their language reveals as much, for it bears a close kinship to Kazak, Kirghiz, and Uzbek.[1]

## ETHNOGENESIS

The legends and folk epics of the Sakhalar tell of military defeats at the hands of the Buryats, a Mongolic people, prompting a northward withdrawal of the tribe with their live-stock into the boreal *taiga,* following the valley of the Lena River. One legend speaks of a progenitor, Elley, descending the Lena in a leather boat or on a raft. This prehistoric retreat of the Yakuts from the steppes into the forested north may have occurred as early as the ninth to thirteenth century or as late as the sixteenth century. Most likely several migra-tion waves occurred. Broad riverine meadows, the gift of annual ice-jam floods, lay along the Lena, and the Yakuts used these grasslands to perpetuate their traditional herding life. Then they discovered the abundant *alases* back away from the streams, another familiar environmental niche.[2]

Through these migrations the ancient ancestors soon reached the lands of the middle Lena, where they created a new ethnic homeland in the eastern reaches of the Central Yakut Plain. Following tributaries such as the Amga and Aldan, they spread through this part of the plain and then moved on to the interfluves in search of *alases.* As the Yakuts occupied this new land, they came into contact and conflict with the native Evenks, a peo-ple of the forest. While the Sakhalar conquered the grassy valleys and lowland plains, using the advantage of their iron weapons, the Evenks, superior bowmen, held on to the thickly wooded plateaus flanking the Yakuts. To this day, the two peoples remain sepa-rated largely by elevation. Upon their arrival, the Sakhalar were a civilized people, possess-ing a system of runic writing, a thirteen-month lunar calendar, metallurgy, domestic live-stock, and a sophisticated cosmology, all of which the Evenks and other native groups lacked. Even so, the Yakuts mixed with the Evenks from an early date, gaining in the process a hybrid identity and knowledge of forest lore that would aid their survival in this hard land.[3]

The formation of a new Yakut identity in the northern homeland did not occur with-out considerable stress. Within a few generations, they lapsed into illiteracy and found that their calendar, fashioned in the heart of Eurasia, did not fit the much colder boreal habitat. But they survived the geographical transition and, equally important, demonstrated a propensity for mixing with other cultures, exchanging ideas and genes, while retaining their identity. They would soon need to demonstrate this skill once more.

## THE RUSSIANS ARE COMING!

Scarcely had the Sakhalar established their homeland when a new intruder, bearing a still more advanced technology, abruptly burst upon the scene. Russian Cossacks, pursuing a fur trade and passage to the Pacific, came to the Lena as explorers and conquerors in the early 1630s, building fortresses that became towns and demanding fur tributes, or *yasak*. While the Yakuts along the Lena initially resisted the Russian conquest, by the middle of the century they had passively adjusted to their new overlords. In fact, the Yakuts flourished, multiplied, and spread geographically under czarist Russian rule. From a population of 30,000 in 1725 they grew to a nation of 227,000 by the late nineteenth century.[4]

With the Russians came many new foods and items of material culture never before known in Sakha—the wheel and cart, sleighs, tobacco, sugar, tea, notched-log construction, cultivated grains, bread, vodka, firearms, and fabric clothing, among others. With them, too, came the Eastern Orthodox Christian faith. Life among the Sakhalar changed forever.[5] In the process of accepting much from Russian culture, while mixing racially with them, the Yakuts steadfastly retained their identity and pride. Vodka, of which Yakuts of both genders became very fond, did not destroy them; nor did Christianity or the Russian language erode their culture. They simply absorbed what they wanted from the Russians and modified their identity accordingly.[6]

The ongoing racial mixing with Evenks and Russians made the Sakhalar a varied people in physical appearance. Some look overtly Mongol, others resemble Central Asian Turks, a few could pass as Japanese, and many appear rather European. Skin hue and eye shape vary. The Yakuts of the Vilyui Bend and Oybon Lake display this mixed appearance, even though they have the reputation of being the purest among their nation. As one elderly woman living at El'gyay on the Vilyui said, "There is no such thing as a pure-blooded Yakut."[7] Their tradition discourages marriage between relatives and places no stigma whatever on unions with Evenks, Evens, or Russians. An American son-in-law was recently accepted with great enthusiasm and celebration, while a Yakutian-speaking American daughter-in-law among the Vilyui Sakhalar has become a national heroine of sorts.

The Russians probably preceded Yakuts into the valley of the Vilyui River. When Cossack explorers first descended the Vilyui to the Lena in 1631, they found Sakhalar only near the mouth of the river, at its confluence with the Lena. The Russians erected three log fortresses at various points along the middle and lower Vilyui, to facilitate the conquest of the local Evenks, the collection of fur tributes, and the use of this river route back to western Siberia and Mother Russia. One of these forts, founded in 1634, would develop into the town of Vilyuisk, while another became the modern Nyurba (Maps 3.1, 3.2). The Russians founded Suntar in 1764.[8]

## THE LEGEND OF DJARKHAN

Evidence is contradictory concerning the time of the Yakut colonization of the Vilyui Bend area. Probably it occurred as early as the 1630s or 1640s, but perhaps later. An official in 1638 noted that only the peoples he called Siniagirs and Nanagirs lived along the Vilyui, and a Russian census taken in the 1670s also detected no Sakhalar in the Vilyui Bend area (Map 3.1). On the other hand, the earliest map of the valley, dating from the 1690s, revealed a dense network of settlements in place by then, some of which bore Yakut names (Map 3.2).[9]

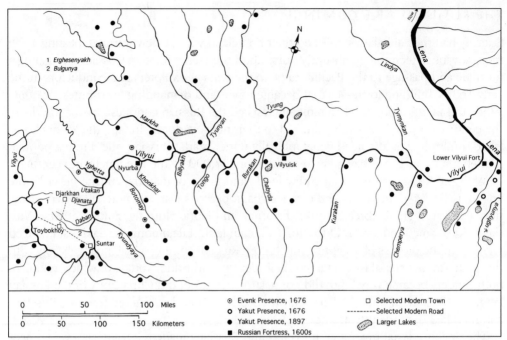

Map 3.1. *The Vilyui River Valley, 1600s to 1900s. Sakhalar settled this region in the enlargement of their homeland, beginning in the 1600s, displacing the native Evenks. A Russian trade route followed the river, defended by three forts. Djarkhan and the roads shown did not exist until the 1930s. (Sources: "Yakutskaya ASSR" 1934; "Russia: Eastern Part" 1996; Jochelson 1934, 220–25.)*

The migration that brought Yakuts to the Vilyui is remembered in the local folklore. These Sakhalar say their ancestors lived along the lower course of the Sinyaya River, a left-bank tributary that flows into the Lena about 200 kilometers (125 miles) south of Yakutsk, in the Kangalas District. Sometime in the middle 1600s, they ascended the Sinyaya westward, crossed a low divide, and descended the Kempendai River to its confluence with the Vilyui at the site of Suntar (Map 1.4).[10]

Perhaps the Yakut occupation of the Vilyui Bend occurred in response to the Russian intrusion along the Lena, as Sakhalar fled up the Sinyaya to escape the fur tribute. One government official in the seventeenth century remarked that, to avoid such taxes, many Yakuts "simply left and there is no information on their whereabouts." The Russians explored and used the Vilyui River route, but it soon lost favor and became an isolated backwater—a good place to seek refuge. Not one among the famous Siberian travelers of the eighteenth and nineteenth centuries journeyed along the Vilyui, choosing instead the Lena route from near Irkutsk and Lake Baikal that the Yakuts themselves originally followed. Still, the traders and tax collectors of Yakutsk by the 1730s knew the Vilyui from mouth to source, and the great bend of the river appeared on maps by that time.[11]

Yakut legend holds that, upon their arrival in the Suntar area, they demanded that the local Evenk chief cede the land to them. The chief pleaded with them to go back where they came from, but the Sakhalar said they could not, because the Russians abused them there. A fight ensued and the Evenks fled the region.[12] Another legend told among the

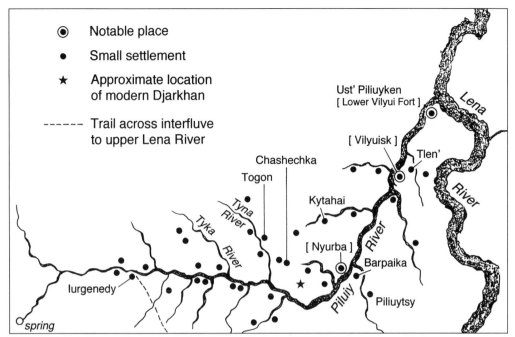

Map 3.2. *Redrawn and simplified version of Remezov's 1690s map of the Vilyui River Valley. Piluiy is the Vilyui, and the rivers Tyna and Tyka are the modern Tyung and Tyukian. Compare to Map 3.1. Numerous settlements appear along the lower and middle course of the Vilyui, suggesting that Yakut colonization had already occurred. The toponyms Togon and Kytahai, for example, reveal Sakha influence. (Source: Remezov 1958, sheet 154.)*

Vilyui Bend Yakuts presents a parallel, somewhat different account of the colonization, and also explains the origin of the name Djarkhan. According to this tale, the Yakut tribe that settled the great bend of the Vilyui bore the name D'Yarkhan or N'Urbagato, appellations preserved in the modern toponyms Nyurba and Djarkhan. They reckoned their descent and derived their name from a woman, variously called Djarkhan or N'Urbakaan. She apparently belonged to a Yakut clan that had attempted to settle at the great bend in the early 1600s, only to be driven away by the Evenks. Fleeing as the lone survivor to the lower Vilyui, she met there a great Yakut chief and warrior, Tygyn, a man reportedly still living at the time the Russians first came to Sakha. The comely Djarkhan became Tygyn's junior wife, a position perhaps merited not just by her legendary beauty, but also by her reputed descent from one of the ancient progenitors of the Yakuts, a man named Darkhan.[13]

Djarkhan bore three sons by Tygyn. As they attained maturity, a dispute arose between Djarkhan and the other, senior wives of Tygyn. She and her sons had to flee for their lives, and after lengthy wandering eventually came back to the great bend of the Vilyui, to the very place Djarkhan had lived earlier. This time her clan conquered the Evenks and established themselves permanently. Abundant meadows along the small streams and numerous grassy *alases* awaited them as the rewards of conquest. The modern Sakhalar living in the *alas* beside Lake Oybon, who perpetuate Djarkhan's name, are in all probability her blood descendants. In fact, the people of Djarkhan village claim to be descended from Yrae Bootur ("Singing Warrior"), the eldest son of Djarkhan.[14]

In this manner, the lands along the middle and lower Vilyui, forming the western reaches of the Central Yakut Plain, became part of an enlarged Yakut homeland. In time, the Vilyuisk *Okrug* (or district) became one of five Russian administrative units within the *Oblast,* or governorate of Yakutia, and by the late nineteenth century, Vilyuisk District was home to nearly 52,000 Sakhalar, a fourth of the entire nation. The district was subdivided into four *uluses* (counties), 56 *naslegs* (precincts or tribal seats), and 244 clans. Suntar, by then the most populous *ulus,* had 14 *naslegs,* 75 clans, and a population of 25,000.[15]

Djarkhan survives as the name of a *nasleg* within Suntar *ulus* to the present day. By 1860, it had been subdivided into three *naslegs,* each still bearing the venerated name. The *alas* where our village stands today belonged by that time to the Second Djarkhan Nasleg, which had 2,223 inhabitants and was the second most populous tribal seat in the entire Vilyuisk District. Nestled within the Second Djarkhan Nasleg, Oybon Lake settlement in 1860 was a mere hamlet, home to only 39 inhabitants, though nearby Arylakh Lake community, on the shores of Ebe, had a population of 127.[16] These two places together can be regarded as ancestral to modern Djarkhan village, though different from it in fundamental ways.

## LAKESIDE HAMLETS

The typical ancestral Yakut rural settlement in the Vilyui Bend area, called a *kystyk,* or winter hamlet, was small and situated beside a lake. The inhabitants of the Second Djarkhan Nasleg in 1860 resided in forty-four different kystyks, with an average of only seven dwellings and fifty-one people in each. Seven of these hamlets had four houses, five others contained five or six dwellings, and six more had only two homes. The largest settlement consisted of only twenty dwellings. Oybon Lake hamlet had six houses and Arylakh Lake had nineteen. That same year, other hamlets near present Djarkhan included Torbos ("Place of the calf") with two dwellings and thirteen inhabitants, Bagana ("Place of the ceremonial pole") with three houses and twenty-three inhabitants, Kilehnkeh ("Glittering waters") with three and twenty-one, Kieng Mar ("Broad marsh") with nine and thirteen, Tyympy with four and twenty-six, Mar-Kyuel with six and fifty, Usun-Kyuel with five and fifty-two, and Tysa-Kys with ten and fifty-eight.[17] This scattering made good ecological sense, as it allowed the Yakuts to disperse through the available grasslands.

Each winter hamlet consisted of a loose row of huts, every one enclosed by individual stockaded fences standing atop earthen berms. The huts bore the ancient Turkic name *yurt,* which had made the transition from "tent" to "winter house" among the Yakuts. Many, called *balagans,* were constructed of palisaded logs in a style probably borrowed from the Evenks (Fig. 3.1).[18] Rectangular in plan, the *balagan* measured 5 to 10 meters (16 to 33 feet) on a side, with a pounded earthen floor excavated to a depth of about a half meter (2 feet). At each corner stood thick vertical timbers, set into the earth and connected at their tops by horizontal crossbeams. Medial posts added more strength. The walls consisted of poles or boards also set into the ground and resting at the top against the crossbeams. All four walls slanted inward in a distinctive, sloping manner. A single, thick ridgebeam—doubled if a sufficiently strong timber could not be found—ran from one side of the hut to the other. Upon this ridgebeam rested poles or boards, birchbark,

Figure 3.1. *Djarkhan cowshed built in the manner of a* balagan. *(Photograph by Bella Bychkova Jordan, 1996.)*

and a layer of earth mixed with clay and cow dung, forming a gently arched, convex roof. In winter, the residents shoveled a layer of snow on top of the roof to improve the insulation. On the slanted walls, a similar plaster was applied, a daubing that required annual repair in the autumn (Fig. 3.2). The *balagan,* when completed, took on the shape of truncated, four-sided pyramid and in winter resembled a bump in the snow. A cowshed of similar design typically abutted the north side of the house, often separated from the living quarters only by a board or skin partition.[19]

A door, made of a single wooden plank covered with cowhide, opened to the east, obeying a Yakut geomancy. Small windows appeared in the southern and western walls, covered by a fish bladder in the summer and by panes of ice in winter. The geographer Ellen Semple noted that the Sakhalar "glaze the windows of their huts with slabs of ice, which are better nonconductors of heat and cold and can be made more perfectly air-tight than glass."[20]

No such houses survive in modern Djarkhan, though some remain in use as cowsheds. Recently, a replica of a *balagan* dwelling was erected as a museum display in the village to remind people of how their ancestors lived. However, as you wander the streets you will see numerous cowsheds built in this old manner. Often, in many different cultures, archaic house types become outbuildings. Among the rural Yakuts this traditional building method and style gradually gave way to Russian-inspired notched-log dwellings (Fig. 3.3). The Sakhalar call this *nyucha djietya,* meaning "Russian house" (Fig. 3.4).[21] Djarkhan today is largely a village of such log cabins.

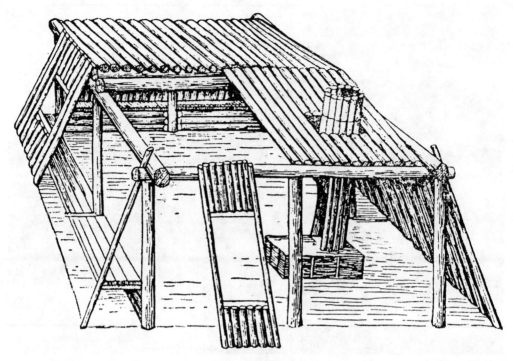

Figure 3.2. *A typical* balagan, *or winter dwelling. Such buildings can still be found in Djarkhan, but only as cowsheds, not houses. (Source: Redrawn and modified from Levin and Potapov 1961, 210.)*

Figure 3.3. *Notched-log building in Djarkhan, displaying a front-gable plan found throughout the subarctic boreal forests, from Norway through Russia, Siberia, and Alaska. It represents Russian influence both in plan and carpentry. (Photograph by Bella Bychkova Jordan, 1996.)*

Figure 3.4. *Venerable log barn that belonged to Danila Tikhonov. He kept milk products here for use in the winter; another part of the shed served as his storehouse. The structure predates Djarkhan's founding and is apparently on its original site, meaning that it survives from the Oybon Lake hamlet of czarist times. (Photograph by Bella Bychkova Jordan, 1996.)*

The lakeside hamlets and huts in the *alases* around present Djarkhan, remote on the interfluve of the Vilyui Bend, enjoyed sufficient isolation from the Russian administrative centers at Suntar and Vilyuisk to permit the survival of much of the traditional Yakut culture into modern times. Not a single Russian resided in the Second Djarkhan Nasleg in 1860.[22] Any who drifted in soon married Yakut women and became acculturated. From perhaps 1650 into the early 1900s, the people of this and neighboring *alases* lived pretty much in the old way. The principal basis of their livelihood was herding.

## A HERDER FOLK

The Sakhalar never abandoned their ancestral Turkic herding system, though some changes occurred after they arrived in the boreal habitat. The horse retained an honored, primary place, prompting Russians initially to call Yakuts "the horse people" (Fig. 3.5). Their language contains many words for the coloration of horses, and Sakhalar reckoned wealth largely in droves of these animals. Horses had accompanied them from the central Asian steppes and later apparently mixed with indigenous Siberian ponies to produce the Yakut breed, splendidly adapted to the colder climate of Yakutia and able to forage all winter out-of-doors without shelter or feed. They "scrape aside the Snow with their Hoofs, to come to the Grass" and "eat the Buds of Birch and Aspen, and grow sleek, plump, and

Figure 3.5. *Yakut horses in an* alas *near Djarkhan, a sight to delight the eye of any native.* (*Photograph by Bella Bychkova Jordan, 1996.*)

fat," marveled a Swedish traveler in the 1720s. Some things never change. Geographer Victor Mote, visiting the Vilyui Bend country in late winter 1985, described how, "in the moonlit pasture, I could faintly see the little Yakutian horses grazing in the clearings they'd created for themselves in the shallow snow," ringed by "circular mounds that hid their fetlocks."[23] These herds are among the northernmost in the entire world, and only a short distance poleward lies the domain of reindeer herding, an activity the Vilyui Sakhalar consistently rejected, regarding it as an enterprise for Evenks, Evens, and Yukagirs. In winter the Yakut horses grow long coats, and the colts become so shaggy as to resemble "long-legged bears."[24] Yakuts traditionally kept four or five times as many horses as cattle, and the minimal desirable herd size for a family consisted of ten to fifteen head, including mainly mares with one stallion, a couple of suckling colts, a yearling, and a two-year-old. Two or three mares were needed for each person in order to yield enough milk, and one or two horses went to slaughter annually for meat. The Sakhalar preferred horseflesh and especially colt meat to any other kind, considering it a delicacy.[25] Horses also served as riding animals and as beasts of burden in pack trains.

Under Russian influence, the number of horses declined, especially in the 1800s, to the advantage of cattle. By 1860 in the Suntar Ulus, 22,728 horses shared the *alases* with 33,795 cattle and 2,341 reindeer. The Second Djarkhan Nasleg about that same time reported 750 horses and 1,385 cattle. The trend toward more cattle continued, and by 1917 Suntar Ulus counted 25,211 cattle and only 7,607 horses.[26] Still, traditions die slowly in the Vilyui Bend, and in the middle 1990s, the new agricultural cooperative at Djarkhan village decided to specialize in horseflesh production.

Figure 3.6. *Cattle drink from a hole chopped in the ice of Oybon Lake, a scene unchanged for centuries. (Photograph by Aleksandra Tikhonova, 1997.)*

Cattle apparently also accompanied Yakuts from the southern steppes, and Russians brought others to Sakha. Cattle survive only with difficulty in Yakutia. They must be stall-fed for eight months each year and lack the hardiness of horses. Cattle, too, live here near their extreme poleward range. The Yakut cattle, "though not remarkably tall, are large, strong, and well proportioned, but the cows do not give a great deal of milk," reported a traveler in the 1820s, and another contemporary observer placed their daily milk yield at 3 to 6 liters (¾ to 1½ gallons).[27]

If not too weakened by the winter confinement, cattle went to pasture about the tenth of May, followed fourteen to seventeen days later by calves and poorer animals. Around September 1, they returned to their stalls at night, but still grazed during the day. After mid-September they remained in the stalls, to be kept on hay for the next eight months, during which time they stopped lactating for at least several months. The Yakuts cut holes in the lake ice and took the cows to drink once each day, a practice still carried on in Djarkhan (Fig. 3.6).[28] Cattle not only provided milk and meat, but also, as oxen, served as beasts of burden. By the nineteenth century, the Vilyui Bend Sakhalar also drove beef cattle to market over a trail leading south from Suntar to gold fields near Olekminsk on the Lena.[29]

Sheep, goats, and camels failed to survive the migration from the central Asian steppes to the *taiga,* and the Yakuts possessed none. When a camel arrived in Yakutsk with a Russian expedition in the 1700s, the local Sakhalar regarded it as a monster and came to stare. The Sakhalar did not have pigs, poultry, or domestic bees, either.[30] An observer in the early nineteenth century "saw neither pigs, sheep, nor poultry amongst them," and in the entire Vilyuisk District, a 1917 census found only four pigs and a like number of sheep.[31] All the poultry in the district belonged to Russian settlers. The Yakuts owned both dogs and cats.[32]

## MILK AND MEAT

Their herd animals yielded essentially a "dairy economy" for the traditional Sakhalar.[33] Milk products ranked first in the Yakut diet, even though mares could be milked only at the beginning of summer. The favorite beverage was fermented mare's milk, or *kumyss,* "an intoxicating, acidulated liquor," of which "they are extravagantly fond."[34] The women made huge quantities of *kumyss* and kept it in barrels made of birch wood. From cow's milk they also produced butter, curds, and *suorat,* a thick yogurt to which they added blueberries, sapwood, roots, and even bones, which dissolved in the lactic acid. They kept *sourat,* which tastes a bit like buttermilk, in large birchbark vats. This milk product provided the most common summer food, and they also stored it in frozen slabs for winter consumption. The Sakhalar traditionally did not make cheese.[35] A herd of about ten cattle supplied a nuclear family adequately with cow's milk.

Though Yakuts had, since the most ancient times, been herders, meat ranked only fourth as an item in their diet. While they dearly loved horseflesh, which is both nutritious and low in cholesterol, and also happily ate beef, they rarely slaughtered either horses or cattle, both because they had only small herds and in order not to diminish milk production. Most livestock they slaughtered were sick. Horse theft for the purpose of acquiring meat was not uncommon, but the perpetrators were usually tracked and apprehended. Meat remained a luxury for most, a food for feasts. Even in the Vilyui Bend, where *alases* were so rich and abundant that large herds could be kept, meat consumption was not all that common and often ceremonial. The Suntar Ulus Sakhalar, for example, consumed the head of the cow ritually. When Yakuts did prepare beef or horseflesh to eat, it was boiled, without salt. They preserved no meat by drying or smoking, though in the winter meat could be frozen. The climate provided a natural refrigerator.[36]

There were other ways to get protein in the diet. The placentas of mares and cows provided a favorite food. Moreover, when a child was born, the father took the afterbirth, and especially the placenta, cooked it, and offered it as a delicacy to his nearest and dearest friends in a celebratory feast.[37]

## HAYMAKING AND TRANSHUMANCE

In Sakha, traditional Turkic pastoral nomadism evolved into a localized transhumance, the seasonal movement of people from the winter hamlet to summer camps, called *saiylyk.* "They shift their habitations," noted a Swedish observer in the eighteenth century, so that the herds would be moved away from the prairies closest to the winter hamlets.[38] The purpose was to prevent depletion of the nearby haymeadows and pastures, so that horses could forage close to the hamlet in winter and also to allow hay to be cut there in late summer.[39]

The summer camps lay from 5 to 50 kilometers (3 to 30 miles) distance from the winter settlement, in uninhabited *alases, yuryakhs,* bogs, and marshes. The sites of many such camps still appear on modern maps of the Djarkhan area. The names of these places are often revealing, as for example Chookar, an Evenk word meaning "Place where grass grows." The summer camps not only served to utilize distant pastures, but also were the scene of feverish haymaking, milking, and milk processing. Beginning in early June and lasting for a month, cows were milked three times daily, and this was also the only period when mares gave milk. When the grasses in the far meadows reached sufficient height to mow, clan judges rode through, allotting space to each family. Hay by the ton was dragged "by oxen yoked to sledges" back to the winter habitations. Ikehr, one of Djarkhan's summer camps in the hintermeadows, means "A place to cut hay."[40]

Near the end of July, the majority of the people and herds returned to the winter settlement, where additional hay was cut. Most of this hay was also brought into the settlements, but some stacks remained in the nearer meadows, and any person belonging to the clan had the right to take some when in need. By the end of summer, huge amounts of hay had been gathered into stacks. The Vilyui Bend area was famous for its hay yields, which permitted greater numbers of cattle to be kept. In the Second Djarkhan Nasleg in the year 1860, for example, the people produced 718 stacks containing a total of 3,500 metric tons (3,850 tons) of hay.[41] Yields fluctuated, however, and the period 1882 to 1885 witnessed a severe decline in hay production in the Vilyui Bend area.[42]

Haymaking developed as a Yakut adjustment to the colder climate, for in ancient times, when they lived as nomads in the southern steppes, they simply followed their herds to new pastures. In Yakut folklore, their former life on the steppes, when no hay had to be cut, was remembered as paradisiacal. In Yakutia, by contrast, the short summer period had to be devoted largely to haymaking. The time of greatest productivity, roughly July, is called *oot yia,* "The month of hay."[43] After hay-cutting had ended, when the frosts deadened the remaining grass, the meadows were often fired.

Early travelers observed natives cutting hay in *alases* and river valleys, using a distinctive Yakut type of short scythe, with a curved handle. "I stopped to see the Yakuts mow grass, which they performed as a man might cut wood in other countries, swinging a short dull scythe above their heads, and literally hewing it down by main strength."[44] The old Yakutian scythe was made of bone and only later of iron. In the late-nineteenth and early-twentieth centuries, it gave way to a longer, more efficient "Russian-Lithuanian" scythe made of steel (Fig. 3.7).[45]

The cutting and gathering of hay required a collective effort, in which the whole family participated. The head of the family usually served as the main hay cutter, assisted by rakers. In one summer such a team could produce 20 to 29 metric tons (22 to 32 tons) of hay, an amount sufficient for twelve to fifteen cattle. The richer members of a clan hired hay cutters, who were paid with food or a modest share of the harvest. These well-to-do families usually remained in the hamlet and did not accompany the others out to the far meadows.[46]

The *saiylyk,* or summer camp settlement, differed in appearance from the *kystyk,* or winter hamlet. It contained a larger number of huts and was more tightly clustered than the winter settlement, usually containing five to ten dwellings. The summerhouse was also of a fundamentally different design. Called an *uraha,* it was conical in shape and tentlike, consisting of nothing more than a birchbark covering over a pole framework.[47] Four to 6 meters (13 to 20 feet) in diameter at the base, the *uraha* was "round, and in the Shape of a Sugar-Loaf," and the birchbark covering was "curiously joint together and embroider'd with Horse-Hair dyed of many Colours."[48] A smoke hole at the top provided ventilation. This design is not traditionally Turkic and seems to have come, with little or no modification, from Evenk hunting shelters. Near the cluster of *urahas* stood the *titik,* or summer calf pen,

Figure 3.7. In these two photographs, Danila Tikhonov sharpens and uses the Lithuanian steel scythe he used to set the all-time Yakutian record for acreage of hay cut daily in a season. Annual competitions, named for him, have failed to equal his record of mowing 86 hectares (213 acres) in one season (Petrov 1992, 130). (Photographs are from the Tikhonov family collection, Djarkhan, taken by A. Timshin, circa 1948.)

to which the cows would come to be milked.[49] Urahas had almost completely vanished by the late 1800s, and no examples exist today, except at the outdoor folk museum near Yakutsk.[50] Camps today have cloth tents instead of urahas (Fig. 3.8).

In modern Djarkhan, very little livestock is taken to the summer pastures. Hay-cutting is now the dominant activity there. When you come upon a camp in the peripheral meadows today, with tents, a fire, and a samovar for tea, it will almost invariably be occupied only by hay cutters (Fig. 3.8). Cattle and horses no longer range far from the village. Even in traditional times, the Vilyui Bend Sakhalar were hardly the "nomads," "seminomads," or "forest nomads," as claimed by many geographers and ethnographers, but instead were transhumants.[51]

## HUNTING AND FISHING

The Sakhalar, herders by ancestry and inclination, relied less on hunting in their livelihood than did other peoples of the boreal forest. Still, they acquired much hunting lore and skill from the Evenks, and Yakut boys married only after they became proficient hunters—a rite of passage that could come as early as age fourteen.[52] Yakut hunters went after diverse, mainly small game, in particular hares, squirrels, foxes (for pelts only), marmots, sable, ducks, geese, partridge, and grouse. In a good year, a hunter could take two hundred

hares, providing winter meat and sparing cattle from slaughter.[53] Duck hunting in the spring and autumn was always a special event for Yakuts, providing an additional food supply. By looking at the spinal bones of the duck, Bella's mother could tell if the summer was going to be dry or wet. While some early observers reported that the Sakhalar would kill and eat just about anything that moved, they in fact had certain taboos. Fox

Figure 3.8. A haying camp in Djarkhan's far meadows today. A tent has replaced the traditional uraha, and livestock no longer come here to pasture. (Photograph by Terry G. Jordan-Bychkov, 1997.)

meat was never eaten, and the killing of swans was believed to bring bad luck.[54] While on the hunt, Yakuts lived in a conical, birchbark hut called an *ityan,* a smaller version of the *uraha* found in summer transhumant camps. It, too, came from the Evenks.[55] The Yakuts loved bear meat, but they both feared and venerated the local brown bear, sharing the circumpolar shamanistic worship of this animal. They would not go after bear in groups of less than twenty hunters, for he was "the master of the *taiga*" in their lore.[56]

Among the weapons they used, the bow and arrow was the most primitive, but it fell out of use after about 1750. The crossbow was still employed to kill hares and foxes in the middle nineteenth century, and rifles came with the Russians (Fig. 3.9). The Sakhalar also knew how to build traps and snares, and game was sometimes driven by horsemen and dogs, a type of hunting believed to have accompanied Yakuts from the steppes.[57] The Yakut hunting dog, foxlike in appearance with a long snout (perhaps helping explain why the Sakhalar would not eat foxes), participated enthusiastically in the hunt, if not always effectively (Figs. 2.16, 5.14). Their greatest shortcoming was a disturbing tendency to run away during the chase and never return. The wealthier men hunted from horseback.[58]

When the Russians came and imposed fur tributes and taxes, Yakut hunting had to be intensified. Almost immediately the hunting ecology was upset. Sable yields in Sakha peaked between 1650 and 1660, followed by centuries of decline. Two hundred years later, no sable or elk remained in the Vilyuisk District, the bear population had been greatly diminished, and the squirrels had deteriorated in quality. As a result, in 1828 the Russians demanded that henceforth taxes in the Vilyui Bend area be paid only in cash. However,

Figure 3.9. *A Djarkhan Yakut ready for the hunt. Note the* balagan *and log house. (Photograph from the Tikhonov family collection, Djarkhan, 1985.)*

furs from the Vilyuisk District continued to reach the Yakutsk market in the 1870s.[59] Russian tributes and rifles made the Sakhalar highly skilled hunters. Bella's grandfather in Djarkhan, Danila Tikhonov, exemplified these skills and could hit a squirrel in the eye with his shot, leaving the pelt intact.

The *alas* lakes around Djarkhan provided abundant fish, especially pike and carp, diversifying the diet and providing needed vitamins, though the Yakuts of the Vilyui Bend had the reputation of eating more meat and less fish than was typical.[60] "As the country inhabited by these people has a vast number of lakes, they never want for fish," reported a traveler around 1825.[61] How did fish get into playa lakes that never drain to the river? A nineteenth-century observer reported that Yakuts brought fish from the streams to stock the lakes.[62]

The Sakhalar fished in the lakes both summer and winter. Near the shore of Ebe Lake, on the outskirts of Djarkhan, we found the ruin of an ancient double dugout canoe once used by fishers, and the local people made horsehair mesh nets (Fig. 3.10). In mid-October, ice fishing began. Recall that Oybon means "A hole cut in the ice for fishing." A sack net called a *munkha* was lowered through the hole to catch fish, which froze almost instantly upon being removed from the water. Ice fishing was, and remains, a collective effort. One group made noise, conveyed through small holes, to drive the fish into the *munkha,* while another teamed pulled the net. The Yakuts probably learned the custom of ice fishing and eating sliced frozen fish from the native Evenks and Evens. Ice fishing lasted into February. If year-round fishing depleted a lake, clan leaders could ban the activity until the waters were restocked.[63]

Figure 3.10. *Ruin of a double dugout canoe, on the shore of Ebe (Arylakh) Lake, Djarkhan. The two dugouts are lashed together. Such boats were once used in summer fishing. (Photograph by Terry G. Jordan-Bychkov, 1997.)*

## THE FRUITS OF THE FOREST

The *taiga* yielded diverse essential foods, and gathering played a major role in the rural Yakut diet. The principal harvest of the forest came in the form of sapwood from pine. In June, the "month of the pine," women went to the woods and cut down young trees, peeled off the layer of new growth, dried it, and ground the sapwood into powder. They then mixed it into the milk products as a sort of flour, and the chemical action of the lactic acid broke down the cellulose fibers. The importance of sapwood in the traditional diet explains why Sakhalar almost invariably settled in the vicinity of pines. Few observers failed to mention this distinctive element of the Yakut diet. The people of the Vilyui Bend area reportedly relied somewhat less on sapwood than other Sakhalar.[64]

Yakut women also gathered wild onions, lilies (used to flavor beverages), wild garlic, and diverse roots. They had used roots for food since ancient times, and must originally have acquired this knowledge in southern Siberia, where natives utilize them in an identical manner. Some roots grew at the bottom of small shallow lakes or in bogs. These were also dried, powdered to the consistency of flour, and added to milk products.[65]

The Sakhalar gathered few berries or mushrooms. They mocked the Evenks, calling them "berry lovers." The women did seek bilberries and red currants, but regarded raspberries as unclean. In Djarkhan the story is told of a woman who brought bilberries to a man to barter for tripe. She felt shortchanged and spread the word of his stinginess through the entire village. A wonderful red currant beverage is part of the Yakuts' summer fare and was already receiving praise from travelers 250 years ago. Yakuts avoided mushrooms and "looked with disgust" when others ate them.[66] Clearly, the Sakhalar never fully accepted the forest and its foods.

Their avoidance of most berries perhaps reflected a fear of bears, who often lurked in berry patches. In Yakut folklore, bears lusted for women and occasionally took them as lovers. If a woman came upon a male bear in the forest, she might protect herself from harm by showing her breasts and shouting, "Kiitim, kiitim!" One Yakut fairy tale tells of a bear who fell in love with a beautiful young woman, abducted her, and carried her away to his den deep in the woods. In time, she bore him a son who became a great warrior.[67] Bears are still feared in Djarkhan today. As a young girl, Bella went with some village women to pick berries, only to flee when they came upon fresh bear tracks.

## TILLING THE SOIL

When Russians arrived in Sakha, they found the Yakuts to be a people who "neither plough, sow, nor plant" and "do not bother to make bread." The idea of tillage, once introduced by the Russians, did not find ready acceptance. A governmental official complained in 1872 that the Sakhalar "really have no desire to sow" and even "view tillage as sinful."[68] By contrast, the Russian settlers in Sakha as early as the 1690s grew grains "in very great abundance," particularly rye.[69] By the 1720s cultivation had become somewhat neglected, perhaps due to periodic crop failures, but a century later the Yakutsk area produced not only grain, but also potatoes, cabbages, turnips, radishes, and cucumbers.[70] Even the Russian efforts eventually diminished, for only 6,475 hectares (16,000 acres) stood under cultivation in all of Yakutia by the end of the nineteenth century, though that area roughly doubled by 1917.[71] Grain harvests remained unimpressive and unreliable, rarely yielding more than five times the amount sown, and some observers concluded that Sakha offered no agricultural promise.[72]

The Vilyuisk District experienced even fewer and later tillage attempts in czarist times. The first cultivation occurred about 1840, among Russians at the town of Vilyuisk, and by 1860 Suntar Ulus had significant grain tillage, both of barley and wheat. The soils were sufficiently fertile, but grain growing in the Vilyui Bend area faced problems of drought, insects, and occasional summer frosts. The local Sakhalar harvested grain with a hay sickle and dried it on slabs of bark, wasting the straw. Reluctant to plow their beloved *alases,* they instead cleared birch and larch forest, an activity they detested.[73] We find no evidence of grain tillage in the *alases* around present Djarkhan in czarist times. The Vilyui Bend Yakuts were the "richest and noblest" of all and saw no need to farm. At most, they would dig ditches to drain lakes and grow hay crops in the dried bed.[74]

In the long run, the Sakhalar accepted only the Slavic vegetable garden, an activity well underway along the Vilyui by the 1860s. In these hoe-tilled gardens the potato reigned supreme, with some attention to cucumbers, cabbage, beets, radishes, carrots, and turnips. The gardens needed frequent watering, requiring ever more people to remain in the lakeside hamlets to tend them during the summer, rather than going to the far meadows and pastures. Melons, cauliflower, and hothouses reached Sakha by the latter half of the nineteenth century, but remained confined to Russian gardens.[75]

The Vilyui Bend Yakuts, then, traditionally pursued diverse food-producing activities, seeking nourishment from the forests, lakes, and prairies. In spite of these strenuous efforts, most rural Sakhalar often or even generally suffered hunger and malnutrition by the end of winter. Famine visited frequently. The Vilyui Bend people fared better than most Yakuts, but even they knew want, sharing what little they had. Life was hard, and we should not portray it as some sort of pastoral idyll.

## TRADITIONAL CRAFTS

The Yakuts came to Sakha bearing such crafts as pottery and metallurgy. They possessed an ancient ceramic tradition, though it remained rather primitive because they did not use pottery wheels, but instead fashioned vessels by hand, using clay from the valleys.[76] From the Evenks and other native forest peoples, the Sakhalar adopted diverse uses of wood and bark, making utensils, crockery, and furnishings. The wood and bark of birch trees were widely used for making wooden vessels, well-known for preserving dairy food products and berries for a long time (Fig. 3.11). They used a special technique that involved the boiling of birch wood prior to carving out a vessel or making a handle for a hunting knife.[77]

From the Russians came carpentry and cabinet-making skills, and the Sakhalar in time excelled at these activities. As early as the 1730s, the Yakuts along the Vilyui had become famous for their furniture making and container manufacture. Bella's grandfather, Danila, still practiced these traditional crafts in the 1960s in a workshop beside his log house.[78]

The Yakuts also worked iron with skill, making arrowpoints, knives, scissors, horseshoes, nails, bridle parts, hay sickles, root diggers, and spark strikers. A blacksmith held high prestige and his position was often hereditary. A ninth-generation blacksmith was considered to possess magical qualities and be as powerful as shamans. The Sakhalar also worked with copper, silver, gold, tin, and lead. In addition, they developed an impressive tradition of jewelry manufacture that survives today.[79]

To make clothing, carpets, and blankets, Yakuts used leather, horsehair, and furs. For softening pelts, they employed a distinctive wooden machine, known as a *talky,* that pressed the fur firmly between opposing rows of teeth. This ancient machine remains in use today (Fig. 3.12). The Sakhalar made fine horsehair carpets and waterproof horse-leather boots.[80]

## TRANSPORTATION

Movement between the lakeside hamlets and the summer camps, hauling of hay from the meadows, the hunt, and journeys to trading posts all required means of transportation. Horses and oxen dragged hay on land sledges, a vehicle also usable in winter (Fig. 3.13).

Figure 3.11. *Traditional containers made of birch, in use in Djarkhan today. The container on the left was made of birchbark; the bowl on the right was carved from a single block of wood. (Photograph by Bella Bychkova Jordan, 1996.)*

Wheeled vehicles of any type were unknown almost everywhere outside of Yakutsk until the early 1900s, as were roads.[81]

Rural Yakuts rode horseback and made saddles of a type similar to those used on the central Asian steppes. They transported furs on packsaddles, using ancient trails. The Sakhalar adopted skis from the aboriginal residents of Yakutia. The bottoms of these wide, short skis were covered with fur, which made them easier to use in the snows of the forest.[82] By whatever device, the Vilyui Yakuts went often to visit other hamlets during the long winter. The snow on the trails between hamlets became packed hard from frequent traffic.[83]

The Vilyui Bend people found travel much more difficult in the summer. They lacked access to the waterways and did not, as a result, make the birchbark canoes widely found elsewhere in Sakha.[84] In any case, the summer was filled with work activities, and they journeyed no farther than the haying camps during that season.

## YAKUT COSMOLOGY AND RELIGION

A leading Yakut chief living at the site of modern Yakutsk very early "embraced the Greek Christian religion," nominally converting the entire tribe, but Eastern Orthodoxy served merely as a veneer beneath which the Sakhalar continued to practice most of their traditional beliefs.[85] In the 1720s, almost a century after the chief's conversion, one European visitor called them "a Pagan people."[86] A pious German traveler in the 1840s reported, disappointed, that while most Yakuts were baptized, they retained nothing of the faith except their Christian names, the pronunciation of which they mangled.[87] In fact, many Sakhalar only converted to Christianity in order to obtain a three-year exemption from taxes and fur tributes.[88] Beyond the limits of the town of Suntar, no church building was

Figure 3.12. *Okdos Pakhomova of Djarkhan uses a* talky, *an ancient toothed device, to soften a fur pelt. Many folk tools remain in use today. (Photograph by Bella Bychkova Jordan, 1996.)*

ever erected in the Vilyui Bend area, and the people of the *alases* remained happily unchurched.[89] As a result, Yakut cosmology and ideas "as to the creation of the world have not been affected by contact with Christianity."[90]

Yakut paganism involved shamanism and animism. The Sakhalar perceived every component of their environment—forests and flowers, rivers, lakes, birds, bears, trees, clouds,

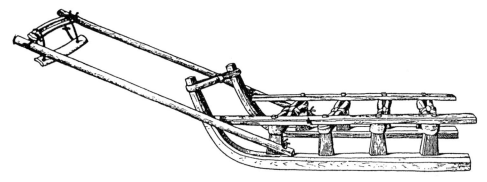

Figure 3.13. *Traditional Yakut land sledge, of the type used in the Djarkhan area. An all-season vehicle, it was drawn by oxen or horses.* (Source: *Modified and simplified from Jochelson 1934, 187.*)

fire, the sun, and moon—as animate entities, each having a spirit. The Lena River was called tenderly Grandma, and the Vilyui, Grandfather. These native spirits could prove troublesome, and holy people—shamans—could exercise some control over them.[91]

All too commonly, we of the West erroneously assume that shamanistic, animistic religions are primitive. In the case of the Sakhalar, however, the religion involved an original, complex, and sophisticated cosmology, recorded in their folkloric epic, *Olonkho*.[92] The Yakuts who dwelled beside Oybon, in common with their nation at large, were a civilized people.

*Olonkho* remained an oral tradition until recorded in written form in the twentieth century. Its core consists of the Yakut cosmology, describing a universe that includes three divisions: the upper world, where gods of creation and prosperity dwell; the middle world, inhabited by living people, the souls of the dead, and various spirits; and the lower world, occupied by demons. The upper gods, creators of the universe and life, are ruled by the White Creator Lord, Ayy-Toyon, who dwells in the highest plane, on the seventh sky in the East. He is dispassionate and does not interest himself with the affairs of mortals. In accepting a veneer of Christianity, the Sakhalar loosely linked Ayy-Toyon to Jesus. By contrast, Uluu-Toyon is a god very much concerned with people. He lives closer to the earth, on the third sky, in the West, an evil cardinal direction. All the virtue in the universe derives from the White Creator Lord. Uluu-Toyon exercises less benevolent functions but is easy to appease. Another powerful being among the pantheon of the deities is the goddess of fertility and plenty, Ayysyt, who comes when a woman delivers a child, bringing a soul from the sky. The Sakhalar believe that sadness and longing for perfection in their hearts are caused by memories of a soul of a better previous life in the upper world.[93]

All good creatures and spirits reside in the East, all the bad or angry ones live in the West, so the Sakhalar normally construct their houses facing east, sometimes north or northeast, but never west. In Djarkhan even today we found the belief that a constantly sick woman is afflicted because her house faces west. A part of traditional Yakut geomancy, this belief concerning the special position of the East apparently derives from an ancient Yakutian cult of the sun. The most sacred celebration of this cult, *ysyakh*, occurred on the day of the summer solstice, the Yakutian New Year. Celebrants chose the most beautiful grassy meadow and erected a ritual post, with symbolic carvings on it (Fig. 3.14). They performed a series of rituals, dedicating the post to the creator gods, and sacrificed a white horse. *Kumyss,* the fermented mare's milk drink, was offered to the gods and then shared

Figure 3.14. *Ritual post erected in 1996 to mark the sixtieth anniversary of the Djarkhan school. Traditional ornaments are carved on the post. On the top is a symbolic vessel (choron) used for drinking* kumyss *during summer festivals. (Photograph by Bella Bychkova Jordan, 1996.)*

with every participant in the celebration. Ysyakh was also a festival featuring various competitions in singing, dancing, jumping, boulder-lifting, wrestling, and racing. It is still enthusiastically celebrated today, though now as a largely secularized event.[94]

The middle world in Yakut cosmology houses people as well as numerous spirits of Nature and the unsatisfied souls of the dead. The spirits vary in their attitude and importance to people. A bear is one of these creatures, possessing a middle world spirit and considered to be a magical, superior being. Its name is never spoken, and the Sakhalar instead call the bear *ehe,* or "Grandfather." Before they consume bear flesh, considered to be an ultimate remedy for almost all diseases, they must say "Huk" three times. Bella's mother told her to do the same thing before she started treating her bronchitis with heated bear fat. The Sakhalar, then, belong to the boreal culture complex of bear ceremonialism found across northern Siberia and across the Bering Strait in Alaska and Canada.

Another spirit who survived both the conversion to Christianity and the communist ideology is Bayanai, lord of the *taiga*. Before they hunt or fish, men make a fire and offer food and drinks to Bayanai. On the whole, the cult of fire was very important in the traditional Yakut system of beliefs. The Yakut admired and feared the power of fire, considering it sacral and regularly offered the hearth spirit, Yot-ichchite, part of their food and drinks. Today even city-dwelling Yakuts holding university diplomas venerate the fire in their gas stoves every time they have guests or celebrations.

Discontented souls of the dead—*örs*—were perceived by the Sakhalar as a problem for the living. When *örs* bothered people, a shaman was called to help, serving as a middleman between people and the world of spirits. Shamans, who often lived apart from others in remote places, were divided among the "white" ones, harmless, and the "black" ones, feared by everyone. The latter could be both good and bad, so a person needed to be very careful to appease them. In fact, only a black shaman could fight an angry spirit, while a white shaman merely appealed to the good gods for favor. As shamans got older and weaker, bad spirits could take revenge on them. Sometimes very powerful and deserving shamans became secondary members of the pantheon.[95] For centuries the lands along the Vilyui have had widely known shamans. The fame of one of these, who reputedly passed a knife through his body without harm, even reached the ear of a German traveler far away on the Lena in the 1730s.[96]

Everything is interconnected in the traditional Yakut universe. Bad is interwoven with good, beautiful and healthy with ugly and sick. That is why a symbolic Tree of Life connects all three worlds. Its roots start in the lower world, inhabited by the demons; its trunk supports the middle world, where people dwell; and its crown reaches the upper world.[97] We should not underestimate the complexity and originality of this cosmology.[98] Though the Yakut mentality bears an imprint of fetishism, it has "achieved an ultimate phase of development" involving a "complex, integrated, and original world outlook, the emergence of which was disturbed only modestly by the establishment of Christianity."[99] In Djarkhan, many traditional beliefs persist, playing a significant role in everyday life and livelihood.

At the same time, many elements of traditional Yakut religion gave way under Russian influence. For example, they formerly disposed of the dead by putting the body in a tree, by abandoning it in the yurt where death occurred, or by cremation.[100] Under Russian influence, even in the remotest hamlets, the Sakhalar began burying their dead and erecting small log huts over the graves in the Russian manner. Many of these little gravehouses survive from prerevolutionary times in the Djarkhan area (Fig. 3.15).

## SOCIETY

A complex cosmology rested upon an equally complicated social structure. Traditionally the Sakhalar lived in clans, or *aga-usa,* the size of which varied considerably, from a few people to several hundreds. Clan membership extended to the ninth generation, after which the people were no longer considered relatives and could intermarry. The size of the

Figure 3.15. *Notched-log burial houses, isolated in a meadow near Djarkhan and dating from prerevolutionary times. The style and construction represent Russian influences. Such structures also reveal the sites of prerevolutionary hamlets. (Photograph by Bella Bychkova Jordan, 1996.)*

clan depended upon birth rate, infant mortality rate, and wealth. Multiple clans formed tribes, such as the D'Yarkhans of the Vilyui Bend area. Clan leaders were male, and women held an inferior position in Yakut society.[101]

Great disparity of wealth existed within the clan. The poorest members owned no livestock and hired their services out to the wealthy. Many worked as servants, but slavery and serfdom never reached Sakha. Even the poorest were free. Food was shared, and if enough existed to go around, nobody starved. In bad years, the closest relatives would be taken care of first.[102] They said, "Why should anyone die when he could eat with his neighbors?" Hospitality was highly developed, for "we know what it is to be hungry."[103]

The Sakhalar had a highly developed sense of private property and owned dwellings, horses, and cattle individually. Most pastures, meadows, and forests remained communal, under the supervision of clan judges, though by the nineteenth century some rich Yakuts had seized and enclosed high quality grasslands.[104] These properties became hereditary, and as one observer noted, "Yakuts know their genealogy well, and land disputes are rare."[105] In communally held prairies, periodic reallotment of haying and grazing rights occurred.[106] As private property rights increased, probably in imitation of the Russian class system and property holding, the clans weakened and died, not surviving into the twentieth century. A census in the 1890s recorded no remaining clan divisions among the Sakhalar.[107] Social stratification was well developed by the time of the Bolshevik Revolution.

In the male-dominated society, polygyny was practiced by affluent Yakuts, who could have up to five wives. Even in monogamous families, children were numerous (Fig. 3.16).[108]

Figure 3.16. *Rare photograph of a Yakut family of the Djarkhan area, about 1904. The widely differing ages of the children in the photograph suggest that other children had died. The clothing is Russian style. (Photograph from the Tikhonov family collection, Djarkhan.)*

Children were regarded as a form of wealth. "For we Yakuts in this icy land," said one peasant, "many children mean more profit than ownership of many livestock and much land." After all, "money will be spent and animals die, while good children will provide for their aged parents."[109]

Five to ten children represented the norm for a woman, and some bore as many as twenty or more, in response to an extremely high infant mortality rate. In the late nineteenth century, astoundingly, only thirty-one children survived to adulthood of every hundred born.[110] Yakut parents worried constantly about the health of their offspring. They believed evil spirits stole the children's lives. A common attempt to outsmart the demons involved making a wooden figure of a baby and burying it in the yard. They hoped after that ritual that the bad spirits would not bother their real baby, thinking it dead. A display of such wooden dolls is housed in the Museum of Regional Studies in Yakutsk.

The twentieth century would bring unprecedented change to these remote *alases,* for there would be no escaping the effects of the Bolshevik Revolution, collectivization, the second World War, and other great events of the century. Lenin, Marx, and Stalin would all pay figurative visits to the settlement beside Oybon.

# 4 · SOVIET VILLAGE

The fateful year 1917 brought the overthrow of czarist rule and the Bolshevik Revolution, but these events had little immediate effect on the Yakuts living on their *alases* within the great bend of the Vilyui River. They continued for a time to live much as their ancestors had, herding cattle and horses in more or less the ancient manner. The Russian Provisional Government had appointed a commissar for Yakutia, and in June 1918, after the Bolsheviks took power, a Soviet regime was proclaimed there. Not until December 1919, more than two years after the Revolution, did the Communist government actually become established in Yakutsk, following suppression of a counterrevolutionary effort, part of the general civil war between "Whites" and "Reds." It required three and a half more years of fighting for the Communists to seize power throughout Sakha.

The Yakutian Autonomous Soviet Socialist Republic was proclaimed in April 1922, before the fighting had ceased, and in December of that year the first All-Yakut Constituent Assembly of Soviets was held. Even these events had little immediate effect on the Sakhalar living beside Lake Oybon. Yakutia's population was 95 percent rural in 1926, and Communism remained initially an urban phenomenon. The lack of a transportation network in Yakutia provided an isolation that initially insulated the hamlet-dwelling herders and hunters. In any case, the first decade of Communist rule was one in which small-scale rural capitalism had free rein.[1]

This isolation ended in the late 1920s, when an extension of the "Old Vilyui Road" westward out of Yakutsk was completed to Nyurba and Suntar. Within a few years, this winter highway reached past Toybokhoy to Krestyakh.[2] With the construction of this national route, the outside world and the Revolution finally came in force to the Lake Oybon Yakuts. The geographer Mark Jefferson, almost exactly at this time, wrote of "civilizing rails," noting the role of railroad construction in the spread of Western Civilization.[3] In rural Sakha, we can paraphrase this as the communizing roads.

## COLLECTIVIZATION

As it happened, Stalin's drive to collectivize Soviet agriculture and eradicate private landownership in the late 1920s, proclaimed in the first Five Year Plan, coincided with the building of the highway across the Vilyui Bend. Collectivization swept through Sakha between 1929 and 1934.[4] In the former year, only 3.6 percent of the households in the Yakutian Autonomous Republic had experienced collectivization, but by 1932—the year of Djarkhan's founding—the proportion had risen to 41.7 percent.[5]

Nine small *kolkhozy,* or collective farms, were established in the Second Djarkhan Nasleg by 1936, including Budyonny, located at Arylakh village—the name Djarkhan bore as late as the 1960s or 1970s. Named for a famous "red" general in the Civil War, Budyonny was but one of 1,160 collective farms in Yakutia by 1940. In theory, the collectives were voluntary producer cooperatives, led by elected officials in a system called "*kolkhoz* democracy."[6]

Collectivization brought hardships for some in the early years, but most rural Yakuts stoically received socialism as just another inevitable Russian idea that had followed the same diffusionary path that earlier brought them Christianity, bread, vodka, rifles, and the wheel. The movement was carried out with a "total disregard for the local peculiarities" of Yakut culture, and some experts, erroneously we feel, attribute the decline in the Yakut population, from 240,500 in 1926 to 236,700 at the 1959 census, to the brutality of the drive for collectivization.[7] One scholar described the resultant crisis in the 1930s, in which many Soviet farmers perished from hunger, as a "harvest of sorrow."[8]

In Arylakh, the disruptions were far less serious. No stories of starvation or murder in this period are known in the village today. Several affluent local families of "Whites" understandably opposed collectivization, but the large majority of people actually stood to gain by it. Kuzma Nikolayev, one of the Arylakh protesters, had his name brought to the attention of authorities in Yakutsk in 1935, but he and the others received no punishment other than having their wealth confiscated, which in any case was inevitable. Verbal abuse remained the extent of repression in Arylakh, and even then the aggrieved parties could and did respond. An ancient Yakut custom, surviving today, involves forming a celebratory circle of people, who dance and chant. Everyone in the circle must repeat the exact words of the chant leader, which are usually benign or humorous. At a Communist Party anniversary celebration, held at Arylakh shortly after collectivization, one of the disgruntled Whites used his turn as chant leader to say, "Things were a lot better before the Communists." Everyone else in the circle had to repeat this blasphemy, creating a local scandal! No punishment ensued. Communism, in this remote place and within the Yakut ethnic setting, generally displayed a rather benign character, closer to the intentions of the Marxist founders, closer to true socialism. The only people here who got "burnt by the sun" just stayed outdoors too long! True, the intrusion of Soviet authority and power had a traumatic aspect, but the local Sakhalar adapted themselves to it. Communism and collectivization were just the latest Russian ideas to arrive by way of the old fur routes.[9]

## BIRTH OF A VILLAGE

The creation of Arylakh and other villages represented one of the most fundamental changes accompanying collectivization. "The construction of settlements was a major achievement in the socialist reconstruction of the Yakutian countryside."[10] All over rural Yakutia, people were obliged to move from small ancestral hamlets into these planned villages, in a process called *poselkovanie,* or "village-making," in Russian.[11] A few remnants of the abandoned, precollective hamlets still exist in the *alases* around Djarkhan, usually in the form of grave houses (Fig. 4.1). In 1932, officials selected the site of the prerevolutionary hamlet of Oybon Lake for the new village, though the name, Arylakh, came from the larger traditional settlement on nearby Ebe Lake. Surveyors quickly staked out the gridiron of broad streets that survives today (Map 4.1). Both Arylakh's checkerboard configuration and lakeside site were typical of Yakutian collective villages.[12] A rigid Russian socialist geometry was added to the long list of unrequested gifts the Sakhalar received from their rulers.

In all such villages, "The center is reserved for the school, collective farm administrative office, medical center, and club."[13] Arylakh developed slowly at first, along the north-south street that today passes in front of Djarkhan's community hall, gym, and

Figure 4.1. *The gravehouse of a wealthy prerevolutionary family, in the meadows north of Djarkhan, is all that remains of a hamlet from the period before collectivization. (Photograph by Bella Bychkova Jordan, 1996.)*

post office. On that same street stands possibly the only in situ structure surviving from the ancestral Oybon Lake hamlet, the venerable Tikhonov log storage barn, at least a century old. It displays its antiquity both architecturally and in its failure to obey the geometry of the surveyor's grid (Map 4.2) (Fig. 3.4).

The village, though new, from the very first had a very traditional appearance (Fig. 4.2). Most of the log houses were not new, but instead were relocated from various hamlets.[14] For example, the Danila Tikhonov house, in which both Bella and her mother Olga were born, was brought to Arylakh village from Kilehnkeh hamlet, south of Oybon, about 1939. The formative hamlet-to-village relocation, in fact, took about a decade to complete. Arylakh developed slowly and its gridiron never filled up fully. By 1939 the village housed a population of 292, over *half* seventeen or younger, and had reached its first growth plateau (Table 4.1). The lands belonging to Arylakh at that time were far less extensive than they are today, and neighboring, since-vanished villages of comparable size, such as Torbos and Chookar, had their own separate identities and collective farms (Map 2.1) (Table 4.1).

The clustering of the Sakhalar into such villages served several purposes. The rural population could more easily by administered and indoctrinated when gathered in larger settlements. But the principal, more beneficial goal was to provide the rural people with services not previously available, such as schools, libraries, power-generator stations, scientific farming and hunting technologies, medical clinics, public health programs,

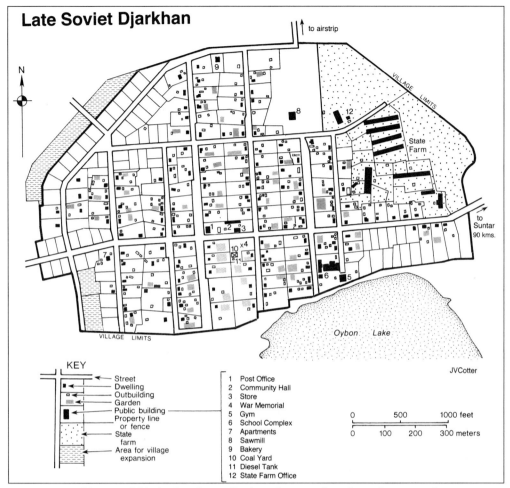

Map 4.1. *Djarkhan/Arylakh developed initially along the central north-south street and never completely filled the gridiron surveyors laid out for it.* (Sources: *Unpublished plan in the village council hall, Djarkhan; interviews with villagers.*)

radio-telephone links, bus transportation connections, stores, and recreational facilities. Djarkhan's school, for example, dates from 1936. These various facilities and services greatly improved the standard of living among rural Yakuts and would not have been possible had the population remained dispersed. We should not forget that a hundred years ago, before Communism and the village structure arrived, over 99 percent of all the Sakhalar were illiterate.[15]

In *kolkhoz* Budyonny, as elsewhere in the Soviet Union, ownership was vested in the state, which leased the land to the collective membership in perpetuity. Rent was paid in the form of agricultural goods. Higher authorities dictated what and how much a *kolkhoz* would produce. Each collective, through its elected leader, delivered an annual share of produce to the state. Every villager owed a specified number of days of labor to the *kolkhoz* each year, and this number increased as the decades passed. The workers shared the surplus, on the basis of the number of workdays performed. The trouble was, surpluses did not often exist, in which case the workers remained unpaid, undermining morale and efficiency. As a result, the *kolkhoz* workers spent more and more effort tending their private

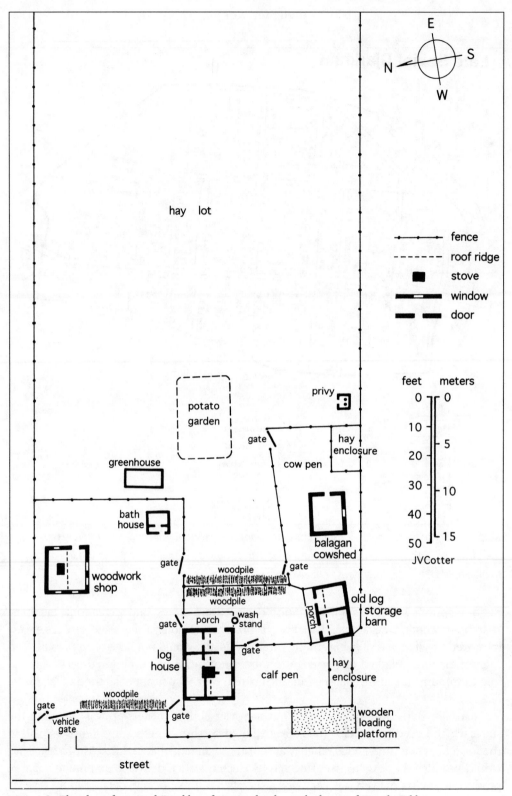

E
N — S
W

fence
roof ridge
stove
window
door

hay    lot

potato
garden

privy

greenhouse

hay
enclosure

gate

cow pen

bath
house

balagan
cowshed

feet    meters
0        0
10
20        5
30       10
40
50       15

JVCotter

woodwork
shop

gate

woodpile

gate

woodpile

old log
storage
barn

porch

porch

gate     porch     wash
                    stand

gate

log
house

calf pen

gate

hay
enclosure

woodpile

gate

gate

vehicle
gate

wooden
loading
platform

street

Map 4.2. *The plan of a typical Djarkhan farmstead—here, the home of Danila Tikhonov.*
*The house was moved here from Kilyankei hamlet about 1939, but the barn is an in situ relic of*
*the prerevolutionary Oybon Lake hamlet. Tikhonov died in 1971, and we have added some elements,*
*observed on other farmsteads, to make it typical of late-Soviet Djarkhan.*

Table 4.1  Population of Arylakh/Djarkhan and Selected Nearby Places

| Year | Arylakh/Djarkhan | Kuosan | Torbos | Chookar | Bes | Kien Maar |
|------|------------------|--------|--------|---------|-----|-----------|
| 1939 | 292 | ? | ? | ? | ? | ? |
| 1941 | 297 | ? | 289 | 342 | 0 | ? |
| 1942 | 300 | ? | ? | ? | ? | ? |
| 1945 | 225 | ? | ? | ? | ? | ? |
| 1950 | 271 | ? | ? | ? | ? | ? |
| 1955 | 220 | 106 | 133 | 125 | 0 | ? |
| 1960 | 302 | ? | ? | ? | ? | ? |
| 1965 | 380 | 160 | 0 | 0 | 0 | ? |
| 1970 | 541 | 92 | 0 | 0 | ? | ? |
| 1975 | 571 | 36 | 0 | 0 | 8 | 5 |
| 1980 | 571 | 8 | 0 | 0 | 0 | ? |
| 1985 | 605 | ? | 0 | 0 | 0 | ? |
| 1991 | 671 | 4 | 0 | 0 | 0 | ? |
| 1997 | 635 | 1 | 0 | 0 | 0 | 4 |

*Sources:* "Demograficheskiye dannye" 1936–67, 1968–83, 1984–99.

plots and their few privately owned livestock, both of which were allowed by the Collective Farmers Charter of 1935.[16] They adopted the widespread Soviet view: "The state pretends to pay us, and we pretend to work."

Several other problems plagued the local collective farms. It became evident very soon that too many *kolkhozy* had been created, requiring local duplication of services and preventing an economy of scale. Consolidation began almost at once. The number of collective farms in the Second Djarkhan Nasleg dropped from nine in 1936 to eight by 1941, six by 1949, and only two by 1951.[17] Arylakh's Budyonny survived all but the last of the consolidations, and it was annexed into the larger Stalin collective in the early 1950s.[18] Collectivization, both in the Vilyui Bend and throughout the Soviet Union, remained basically a trial-and-error process, a grand experiment never before attempted.

## THE GREAT PATRIOTIC WAR

The grand experiment was cruelly interrupted by World War II. Though the Vilyui Bend villages lay far from the theaters of the "Great Patriotic War," their people would suffer great hardships and even death. From the Second Djarkhan Nasleg, which had 1,992 inhabitants in 1941, 99 went away to war, and of these 59 perished. A war memorial bearing a depressingly high number of names stands in front of Djarkhan's village council hall today to commemorate the fallen ones (Fig. 4.3). Those who remained in the villages also suffered. In 1942, a "military tax" was imposed on Yakut farmers. Many farmers had to sell some of their privately owned milk cows to pay the tax, and the loss of the cows often

Figure 4.2. *Street scene in Arylakh/Djarkhan village, about 1948. The settlement, though only fifteen years old, had a traditional appearance. Most houses had been moved here from nearby pre-revolutionary hamlets. (Photograph by A. Timshin, from the Tikhonov family collection, Djarkhan.)*

Figure 4.3. *The memorial to those who died in the Great Patriotic War is topped by a red star and stands in front of Djarkhan's village council hall. (Photograph by Bella Bychkova Jordan, 1996.)*

left families hungry or starving. A drought in the summer of 1942 and severe winter in 1943–1944 deepened the local crisis. In 1943, the Soviet government finally distributed some cattle to the families of soldiers at the front, but many still faced hunger. As the decisive months in the war effort approached, the slogan "Everything for Victory" exhorted the villagers to give still more. Some people at Torbos and Chookar villages died of starvation during this time and immediately after the war. In Yakutia at large, the rural population shrank from 301,000 in 1939 to 211,000 by the end of the war, a decline of 30 percent. Arylakh's population decreased by 67 persons, or 23 percent, in that period (Table 4.1).[19]

Remarkably, not one of the residents of Arylakh starved, due in large part to the compassion and skill of the Budyonny *kolkhoz* leader, Comrade Pakhomov, the grandfather of the present chairman of the Sakha Committee for Land Reform. On his own initiative, he distributed the collective's seed grain to starving families, even though such an action was a capital offense in Stalin's time. Luckily, the party officials in Suntar never found out, and everyone survived that cruel winter of 1943–1944.[20]

Bella's grandfather, Danila Tikhonov (Fig. 4.4), was one of the wartime officials of Budyonny, and he, too, acted compassionately in the food crisis. One day an emaciated teenager named Moisey Ivanov stole a fresh cowhide, with some meat clinging to it, from Danila's farmstead fence and dragged it home to a small house on the edge of Arylakh, where his mother lay ill and near starvation, her husband away at war. For the boy and his mother, the cowhide meant life. Danila easily tracked Moisey's trail in the snow and came to their house. The boy watched in fear, hiding behind the stove, as Danila entered the house and talked to his mother. He could not hear the conversation but could only see the sad expression on Tikhonov's face as he smoked his pipe and listened. Danila left without reclaiming the cowhide or even chastising Moisey. The next day, after dark, Danila rode by their house and threw a sack of bran over the fence. Moisey and his mother survived the winter, and many years later, long after Danila died, Moisey Ivanov told the story to Bella. He, incidentally, went on to a distinguished career in the Soviet military and later with the KGB. Today, a pensioner, he spends summers in Djarkhan.

These stories serve to put a "human face" on socialist Djarkhan. Even in the darkest Stalinist times, local leaders and villagers acted with compassion, initiative, and intelligence, though at personal risk. Ancient Yakut ways persisted in the face of the distant tyranny, strengthening the sense of community in the village.

## WHEAT FOR COMRADE STALIN

In view of the disruptions and hardships caused by the collectivization process and Great Patriotic War, the Sakhalar of Arylakh village and Budyonny collective farm accomplished simply astounding feats in the 1930s and 1940s. Collectivization brought a huge expansion of tilled land in Yakutia, and the cultivated area increased by two and a half times its size between 1917 and 1946, reaching a total of 92,000 hectares (227,000 acres) in the republic.[21] Budyonny would participate in the expansion. It represented the final attempt by the Russians to make tillers of the Yakuts.

The official policy, dictated by Stalin himself in the 1930s, was to grow small grains, even beyond 60° latitude. Budyonny became an experimental farm in this remarkable endeavor. Comrade Stalin said to raise polar grains, and the Arylakh farmers complied. By 1940 they had 110 hectares (272 acres) of land planted to grains, including 35 hectares

Figure 4.4. *Danila Tikhonov, circa 1948, elected leader of Budyonny collective in the* alas *near Djarkhan. He was Yakutia's champion hay cutter and a skilled furniture maker. (Photograph by A. Timshin, from the Tikhonov family collection, Djarkhan.)*

each of rye and barley, 21 of oats, and 19 of wheat.[22] Arylakh's fields lay in the fertile *alases,* scattered in different locations where the soil was judged best.

Machinery was initially not available, and the Budyonny farmers harvested grain with sickles, working long hours to gather a modest crop. Olga, Bella's mother, recalled how the village children helped by picking up loose kernels in the field after the adults had completed their work. Moisey Ivanov even remembers searching in vain for kernels in mice nests, since everyone believed the rodents pilfered and stored grain. The collective turned over a large share of the grain harvest to the state, then distributed the remainder to the members of the *kolkhoz,* who used crude handmills to make flour.

Arylakh achieved great grain glory in the late 1940s, when Danila Tikhonov, by then the elected leader of the collective, was summoned to bring sheaves of the village's boreal wheat to the All-Soviet Exhibition of People's Economic Achievements, held at the fairgrounds on the outskirts of Moscow. Perhaps this was the village's finest hour. Danila undertook this journey across six time zones to Moscow even though he knew no Russian. A photograph of him with the sheaves is lovingly preserved by the extended Tikhonov family (Fig. 4.5).[23]

By 1950 the grainfields of Arylakh had been reduced to 82.5 hectares (204 acres), 78 percent of which was planted in spring grains and, astoundingly, the remainder in winter grains. It had become apparent that grain harvests were unreliable, with total crop failure occurring in some years. Viewing a dead grainfield, the villagers reputedly indulged in a sarcastic verbal tribute: "Comrade Stalin is a great agronomist." In the year of Stalin's death, Arylakh's fields yielded only 2.2 centners of grain per hectare (196 pounds per acre), whereas six to seven times that yield is required to break even financially. Stalin and his dream essentially died together. In the best year recorded, 1965, the grain yield was still only 8.2 centners per hectare. By the end of the Soviet period, grain cultivation had been abandoned.[24]

Just after World War II, more flour reached Arylakh from America than from the collective's fields. Surplus lend-lease shipments, mainly sacked flour and boots, arrived in the village by truck and were distributed to the astonished members of the collective. Olga Tikhonova recalled fondly how delicious the food prepared with American flour tasted, coming as it did at the end of the time of hunger.

More enduring and successful were Budyonny's efforts in potato and vegetable raising. By 1940 the collective had two hectares of potatoes under cultivation. Soon this venture moved largely to private household gardens, where potatoes thrive to the present day, as do diverse greenhouse vegetables (Fig. 4.6).[25] Bella's great-grandmother even raised chili peppers in her home garden, perhaps the northernmost ever cultivated! This completed the diffusion of the Slavic vegetable garden to the Vilyui Sakhalar, a process begun in late czarist times.

## HAYING AND HERDING

Budyonny Collective Farm also preserved traditional enterprises, in particular raising horses and cattle, providing hay for them, and producing milk and meat. Moreover, a substantial part of this activity was never collectivized, remaining in private hands. In 1941, Arylakh village had 508 cattle, over two-thirds of them privately owned, and 165 horses, three-quarters belonging to the collective (Table 4.2). Huge, elongated cattle barns, built in the style if not the scale of Yakut *balagans,* filled the eastern end of Arylakh, in the collective farm complex. Budyonny also experimented early with a herd of twenty-one reindeer, a venture doomed to failure, since the Vilyui Bend Yakuts regarded them as livestock fit only for Evens, Evenks, or Yukagirs. By 1950 reindeer had virtually disappeared, and the cattle-horse ratio had shifted even more in favor of bovines (Table 4.2). Most cows remained privately owned. Among the persons possessing cattle at mid-century, 63 percent had only a single animal, while another 32 percent owned two. No one in the village owned more than four cows. Collectivization had distributed the wealth, destroying the class distinctions between rich and poor.[26]

Figure 4.5. Danila in the Bear's Den, circa 1949. As collective leader, Danila Tikhonov stands in front of precious sheaves of grain, Arylakh's boreal wheat, at the All-Soviet Exhibition of People's Economic Achievements in Moscow. (Photograph from the Tikhonov family collection, Djarkhan.)

Budyonny collective also established the first modern veterinary medical services ever known beside Lake Oybon and began the process of upgrading the native cattle breed to enhance milk and beef production. Cattle anthrax was eliminated. In the collectivized system, the seasonal migration to summer pastures and meadows survived, but only a designated group of hay cutters and herders went, while most of the people remained in the village to tend the gardens and fields.[27]

Figure 4.6. *Tomatoes and cucumbers growing in a Djarkhan hothouse. Such horticulture, introduced during Soviet times, has been very successful. (Photograph by Bella Bychkova Jordan, 1996.)*

One of the principal goals of the Soviet collective system in Yakutia was to increase hay yields in order to allow larger cattle herds. In many villages, new meadows and pastures were created through forest clearance, but that apparently did not happen around Arylakh, where *alases* are so expansive. By 1949 Budyonny produced 4,290 metric tons of hay, as well as 350 metric tons of silage crops and straw.

**Table 4.2 Livestock Holdings**

| Year | Cattle | Percent Privately Owned | Horses | Percent Privately Owned | Swine | Percent Privately Owned | Reindeer | Percent Privately Owned | Poultry | Percent Privately Owned |
|---|---|---|---|---|---|---|---|---|---|---|
| 1941 | 508 | 69 | 165 | 25 | 0 | – | 21 | 100 | – | – |
| 1950 | 699 | 66 | 145 | 0 | 0 | – | 1 | 100 | – | – |
| 1960 | 2,473 | 27 | 615 | 0 | 52 | 100 | 0 | – | – | – |
| 1966 | 2,210 | 31 | 610 | 0 | 41 | 100 | 0 | – | 209 | 100 |
| 1971 | 1,835 | 23 | 584 | 0.5 | 12 | 100 | 0 | – | – | – |
| 1991 | 530 | – | 862 | – | 65 | 100 | 0 | – | 38 | 100 |
| 1997 | 897[1,2] | 100 | 549[2] | 13 | 0[3] | – | 0 | – | – | – |
| 1999 | 888[2] | 100 | 394[2] | 100 | 0[3] | – | – | – | 273 | 100 |

*Source:* "Demograficheskiye dannye" 1936–67; 1968–83; 1984–99.

*Note:* The changing boundaries of the *nasleg* compromise the comparability of these data: 1941, 1950 = Budyonny *kolkhoz*; 1960, 1966 = Djarkhan *nasleg* of the Lenin *kolkhoz*; 1971 = Djarkhan *nasleg* of Toybokhoy *sovkhoz*; 1991, 1997, 1999 = Djarkhan village and Kuosan hamlet and Kien Maar hamlet.

[1] Of these, 135 head owned by independent peasant farmers.

[2] Underreported to evade taxes.

[3] Count taken January 1, after swine slaughtered.

Figure 4.7. *May Day celebration at Suntar in the late 1940s. Comrade Stalin never visited the Vilyui Bend, but his likeness, name, and directives did. Representatives of Arylakh's Budyonny collective attended the festivities. (Photograph from the Tikhonov family collection, Djarkhan, circa 1949.)*

Immediately following World War II, Soviet officials organized hay-cutting competitions in Yakutia, in an effort to promote increased production. Bella's formidable grandfather, Danila, won that competition, as mentioned in chapter 3. This feat even merited mention in Petrov's period history of the Republic. "The haycutter D. A. Tikhonov of 'Budyonny' collective in the Suntar Region cut by hand 86 hectares of hay during a single season, averaging 2.08 hectares daily," over four times the amount normally cut.[28] Danila's record still stands. These regional competitions were revived in the late 1980s and named for Danila Tikhonov.

## THE LATE COLLECTIVE PERIOD

Around 1952, the surviving collective farms of the Second Djarkhan Nasleg, including Budyonny, merged to form the expansive Stalin *kolkhoz* (Fig. 4.7).[29] In spite of the well-nigh heroic efforts of the Yakuts at Arylakh and other villages, the collective farm sector had continued to perform poorly, especially in the "marginal lands" of regions such as Sakha. State agrarian planners continued to promote collective mergers in their futile quest for a scale economy.[30] The new collective was renamed Lenin in the middle 1950s, and by the time of its demise, in 1966, it encompassed the seven villages of Arylakh, Usun-Kyuel, Mar-Kyuel, Allanga, Toybokhoy, Krestyakh, and Kokunu, as well as numerous smaller places, embracing the western two-thirds of the Vilyui Bend region.[31]

This final phase of collective farm mergers was paralleled in the 1950s by a second episode of settlement consolidation. The number of villages declined. Torbos and Chookar, sizable villages with their own identities, collectives, schools, and amenities, were abandoned during the time of the Lenin collective, and their inhabitants moved to Arylakh, whose population leaped to 380 by 1965, and to nearby Kuosan (Table 4.1).[32]

This second episode of drawing people into larger settlements exacerbated a problem inherent in the original hamlet-to-village movement of the 1930s. The rural resource base of the Vilyui Bend—the *alas* meadows and pastures—exhibits a highly scattered pattern. The Sakhalar of old had responded correctly by scattering through the countryside in hamlets. A dispersed resource is best exploited by dispersed settlement. Every time the socialist planners, seeking the economy of scale, dictated another phase of settlement consolidation, they decreased the access and increased the travel time to the grasslands.[33]

Concentration in sizable villages brought an additional problem, one that continues to plague Djarkhan today: localized forest depletion for firewood. Each dwelling requires huge amounts of stove wood for the winter. In former times, when the population lived dispersed in hamlets, wood was fetched from a larger expanse of *taiga,* but in the village era fuel comes disproportionately from the immediate environs, to the extent that forest damage is evident. The Djarkhan villagers, for thirty years or more, have been burning more wood than the taiga can grow.

On the positive side, the Lenin collective achieved a noteworthy level of modernization. Tractors, which enjoyed an almost religious status in Soviet agriculture, reached Arylakh as early as the 1930s. When the first tractor rolled through the dirt streets, some villagers, who had never seen machines of any kind, mistook it for a devil from the Yakut cosmology and hid in cellars, not venturing out for days.

By the time of the Stalin and Lenin *kolkhoz,* machines of various sorts, including trucks, grain and silage combines, tractors, seeders, and hay mowers became available. Initially, the collective had to rent these machines from a state-owned Machine Tractor Station (MTS), but in the late 1950s the Lenin *kolkhoz,* along with all other collectives, purchased —not without financial hardship—these machines and the MTS was abolished. All of Yakutia had some twenty thousand farm machines by 1960. When disbanded in 1966, the seven villages of Lenin collective owned seventy-seven tractors, twenty-five trucks, and nine combines and mowers.[34]

Electricity first came to Arylakh in 1954, with the installation of a small diesel generator. Only limited hours of electric power were available, even after several larger generators arrived in the 1960s. Cheap, abundant power came in the 1980s, when transmission wires connected the village to a hydroelectric facility on the Vilyui.[35]

By the middle 1960s, "an efficient flying doctor service" had become available, enhancing health care.[36] Another welcome gift from the sky came when a disabled Soviet weather balloon crashed near Arylakh in 1965, like a present from Ayy-Toyon in the seventh plane of heaven above. The villagers, happily ignoring the "Do Not Touch" admonition printed on the balloon, a warning frantically echoed by the leader of the local governing council, literally carried away every fragment of the balloon, particularly prizing the strong nylon ropes and pretty fabric. Within hours, not a trace remained. When authorities arrived by airplane looking for the downed balloon, the villagers declared they had never seen such a thing.

Of even greater benefit to the village were the agrarian economic reforms, begun under Nikita Khrushchev, by which prices for farm produce greatly increased. Even more beneficial, the collective farm workers began receiving cash wages instead of sharecropping. These changes continued after Khrushchev's ouster, culminating in Brezhnev's economic reforms of 1965, which raised various food prices by 70 percent, transforming the rural economy. Collectives in marginal areas such as Sakha received special additional "northern benefits," including price and salary subsidies.[37] Essentially, these reforms ended the long period during which the agricultural sector was bled and penalized to fund Soviet war efforts and industrialization. Subsidies now flowed to the farmers, and no longer were profits skimmed from the villages.[38] This enlightened policy, though very costly, ushered in Djarkhan's golden age.

## THE GOLDEN AGE, 1966–1991

Accompanying the reforms was a final reorganization of the farming structure in the Vilyui Bend area. The Lenin collective gave way in 1966 to a state farm, or *sovkhoz,* named Toybokhoyskiy, after the principal agro-town of the Vilyui Bend that also served as its head-quarters (Map 2.2). Toybokhoyskiy, one of seven state farms created in Suntar Ulus, included only five main villages, fewer than its predecessor, Lenin *kolkhoz.* Clearly, the "bigger is better" policy had been discarded. Rather, the transition to the *sovkhoz* system represented a basic reorganization and restructuring with the aim of establishing a centralized state-owned agribusiness economy.[39] Salaries rose significantly in the late 1960s, and state price subsidies for agriculture increased seventeenfold between 1965 and 1989.[40]

Ignoring the inherent problem of access to grasslands, planners perpetuated the venerable process of settlement consolidation in the *sovkhoz* era. Once again Arylakh village benefited from this cannibalistic process, leaping to a second growth plateau and entering its demographic golden age (Table 4.1). The government decided to relocate, gradually, all 160 residents of Kuosan, as well as the inhabitants of smaller places like Bes, to Arylakh (Map 2.1). The population consequently leaped to 541 by 1970 (Table 4.1).[41] None of these new residents of Arylakh were housed in the barracks or apartment-style housing associated in the Western mind with Russian state farms. Throughout Djarkhan's history, the villagers have lived in their separate, privately owned log homes, which passed by inheritance from generation to generation. In most cases, the houses of the Kuosan settlers were simply moved to Arylakh.

Natural increase also augmented the village population. In Sakha at large, the rural population grew by 71,000, or 25 percent, between 1972 and 1989, virtually all by natural increase, and Arylakh reflected this trend. By 1988, 31 percent of the village's people were aged seventeen or younger, up from 27 percent in 1970. In the latter year, near the end of the Soviet period, almost one-fifth of Djarkhan's population had not yet reached seven years of age![42]

In this episode of rapid demographic growth, the village finally assumed its present name, Djarkhan, though Soviet topographic quadrangle maps continued to label the place Arylakh in the 1970s and 1980s (as did American military intelligence—what *would* the United States Army have done if as a result our troops had been unable to find Djarkhan?).[43] The local people today give somewhat confused and contradictory accounts of the double name, but the change from Arylakh to Djarkhan fits the known demographic events very nicely. In the late 1960s, Mar-Kyuel—a village east of Arylakh—was removed from the Second Djarkhan Nasleg, and this, coupled with the abandonment of Kuosan, made Arylakh the only remaining village in the *nasleg*. The village and administrative unit became synonymous.[44] If pressed, some villagers say that Djarkhan is the name of the village lands or area, while Arylakh is the settlement. In any case, the tall placard at the entrance to the village today bears only the inscription DJARKHAN, and nobody uses Arylakh anymore, except the post office. Oddly, that venerable Yakut toponym was discarded for both the village and the large lake just northwest of the settlement.

## A MODERN PLACE

A golden age connotes a better life, and Djarkhan acquired some rather substantial amenities and new technologies in the late Soviet period. It became a surprisingly modern place, considering its remote location, a far cry from the village where people once fled in fear from devil-tractors.

Among the new amenities were round-trip flights once or twice a week between Djarkhan's meadow landing strip and Suntar, 60 air kilometers (37 miles) away. The schedule was irregular, and the arrival of the small Aeroflot plane invariably generated excitement in the village. The children, including Bella when she visited, had their ears pricked to hear the first droning sounds of the airplane's engine. It was an honor to be the first to report the news, so they ran like the wind to tell the adults, who jumped on motorcycles and rushed to the airstrip, carrying mail, milk samples for testing in Suntar, and passengers. The pilot kept the engine running and would not remain long on the ground before beginning the return flight. Those too slow to get to the airstrip on short notice would camp out in a log cabin "terminal" near where the plane landed, often waiting for days. Some pretended they needed to go to Suntar for some important reason as an excuse to get out of work at the state farm. They leisurely lay in the grass or huddled by the stove, depending on the weather, drank tea, told stories, and played cards, silently hoping that the plane would not come that day. Far less glamorous but more predictable if the road was passable, the weekly bus to Suntar offered another way to get to town. Djarkhan's amenities also included visits by touring theatrical and musical groups, whose performances at the community hall were eagerly awaited and enthusiastically received (Fig. 4.8). Movies were shown there, too, usually once a week.

Djarkhan villagers ate and dressed better than ever before (Fig. 4.9). Excellent Soviet champagne sometimes reached the state store next door to the community hall, and shopping trips to Suntar provided another opportunity to spend one's wages. Sanitary conditions also improved, as did nutrition and medical care. The average lifespan increased in the village and the infant mortality rate declined, prompting the population explosion of the 1980s. A medical survey of three thousand inhabitants of the Vilyui River Valley conducted in late Soviet times revealed lingering health problems linked to the infamous 1961 hydrogen bomb test, mentioned in chapter 1, as well as to pollution of the river and other environmental problems, but we could find no evidence of such illnesses in Djarkhan. Reputedly, the Vilyui Sakhalar suffer genetic and immune-system disorders, but if so, our villagers seem to have been spared. By almost any standard, the people of Djarkhan in late Soviet times were healthy, literate, well nourished, nicely dressed, amply entertained, and contented with their lives (Fig. 4.10). They had money in their purses and places to spend it. The socialist experiment, it seemed, had succeeded, improbably and spectacularly, in this remote boreal place.[45]

Figure 4.8. *A touring concert troupe at Djarkhan's community hall. Such performances were one of the amenities of the Soviet period. (Photograph from the Tikhonov family collection, Djarkhan, circa 1975.)*

Figure 4.9. *Let the good times roll! A celebration in a Djarkhan home in late Soviet times. The standard of living during that period left little to be desired. (Photograph from the Tikhonov family collection, Djarkhan, 1979.)*

Figure 4.10. *Well dressed, healthy, and good-looking; by the late 1970s, the Yakuts of the Vilyui Bend lived well. (Photograph from the Tikhonov family collection, Djarkhan, 1979.)*

Moreover, some basic personal freedoms accompanied the new prosperity. Under the old *kolkhoz* system, the farm workers of Djarkhan remained bound to the land like serfs, with no right to move away. They did not possess internal passports. An elderly aunt who still lives in Djarkhan told Bella that, as a result, some people did not even know their age, and when time came to retire, they could not prove their eligibility for pensions. The aunt was among those. She failed to demonstrate her age and had to work an extra five years before she could retire with a pension. In the *kolkhoz* era, graduates of the local school could not leave the village for college before working for three to five years at the collective farm. Only two or three of the best students were allowed to seek higher education in Yakutsk. Bella's mother graduated from school with honors, becoming one of the rare *kolkhoz*-era emigrants.

In *sovkhoz* times the villagers obtained internal passports and could leave Djarkhan to seek their fortune elsewhere if they wished. After 1985, with Gorbachev's liberalizing reforms, migration became even more common, causing Djarkhan's population to fluctuate wildly. In 1985 the number of inhabitants stood at 605, which plummeted to 500 the next year and then rocketed up to 687 in 1987.[46]

The new freedoms also allowed more private initiative. One villager, who Bella knew simply as Uncle Savva, acquired five cows, a bull, and several horses by the early 1970s, enough to be called a rich man by the other villagers. He was hard-working and clever. In another age he would have been a *kulak*—a well-to-do peasant.

Mostly these years proved uneventful. Some excitement ensued when the level of Oybon Lake rose higher than usual in the late 1970s and early 1980s, threatening to flood the edge of the village. An ambitious plan was put forth, relying upon traditional Yakut channel-digging practices, to drain the excess water north through the woods and into Kelteghey Lake, whose waters lie 5.6 meters (18.3 feet) below Oybon (Fig. 4.11). Teams of *sovkhoz* workers armed with picks and shovels dug the channel, but for some reason it did not work, perhaps mainly because Oybon's level receded of its own accord. Villagers still shake their heads in puzzlement over what went wrong and caused so much hard labor to be wasted. Next to the abandonment of grain farming, the great drainage canal fiasco probably represents Djarkhan's greatest socialist failure, not that anyone lost much sleep over it. The mounds of excavated earth from the project will probably remain an archaeological curiosity ten thousand years from now. "Civilized if occasionally misguided people lived here," will be the message of the mounds.

## PRODUCING MEAT AND MILK

The state farm operations were more specialized and commercialized than the old collectives'. Gone were the ill-advised experiments with wheat and reindeer. Toybokhoyskiy simply fell back upon the traditional Yakut specialties—beef, horseflesh, and milk, with hay and fodder to feed the cattle. The main thrust involved converting the traditional system into a modern, efficient, mechanized, commercialized agribusiness. Not too far west by road lay the new diamond-mining center of Mirny, a promising market. Toybokhoyskiy *sovkhoz* would help feed that emerging metropolis, as well as the county seat, Suntar.[47]

Production levels in Toybokhoyskiy increased, spurred by the investments of the Soviet state. Brezhnev's Nonchernozem Zone Program after 1976 provided still larger subsidies. Djarkhan's division of the *sovkhoz* did its part. In 1971, the village produced 1,160 centners of beef (128 tons) and 297 centners (33 tons) of horseflesh, 112 percent of the previous year's output. Feed production included 9,822 centners of hay (967 tons), 92 (9 tons) of straw, 300 (30 tons) of silage, and 536 (53 tons) of fodder concentrate. The state farm's 542 cows at Djarkhan in 1971 gave 1,322 kilos (2,908 pounds) of milk. Livestock increased in number, especially between 1981 and 1986. Herd upgrading continued, crossing exotic Simmental and Kholmogor dairy breeds with the Yakut cows in a way that retained the high butterfat content and hardiness of the native while increasing yield. By the 1980s some cows were milked by machine at Djarkhan.[48]

Figure 4.11. *Work crew from the Djarkhan division of Toybokhoyskiy* sovkhoz *assigned to dig a drainage channel between Oybon and Kelteghey Lakes. The channel, for some reason, did not function. (Photograph from the Tikhonov family collection, Djarkhan, circa 1980.)*

Still, not all was well in the *sovkhoz* system, either locally or nationally. In effect, the government was financially overextended, paying far more in agriculture subsidies than it could afford, in spite of increased yields. Costs soared much faster than productivity. Also, demand for agricultural produce outpaced supply, due to the improved diet and rising living standards of the Soviet people, but the government would not permit food prices to rise accordingly. Bad harvests in several regions of European Russia in the early 1980s deepened the agrarian crisis.[49] Forces residing far away from Djarkhan and Toybokhoyskiy *sovkhoz* would soon end, as they had initiated, the brief rural golden age. The entire Soviet economic and political system teetered toward collapse.

## TWILIGHT AT TOYBOKHOYSKIY

Outwardly, no crisis seemed imminent in the 1980s. Certainly the villagers had no inkling of what was coming. The last decade of the Soviet Union is fondly remembered as a good time in Djarkhan (Fig. 4.12). As it happened, a wandering German geographer, Norbert Wein, passed through Toybokhoyskiy state farm in 1989, recording what he saw and heard, unaware that the *sovkhoz* neared the end of its days. He wrote an account, Teutonically detailed and factual, providing a fitting epitaph and eulogy for the enterprise.[50] Toybokhoyskiy, the largest state farms in Suntar *ulus*, impressed Wein, not unreasonably, as a going agribusiness concern. It consisted of about 36,000 hectares (89,000

Figure 4.12. *Happy days in the setting Soviet sun: a high school graduation celebration in the alases near Djarkhan. (Photograph from the Tikhonov family collection, Djarkhan, 1990.)*

acres) of land, three-quarters of which could be used for agriculture with the remaining quarter covered by *taiga*. Natural meadows occupied 16,400 hectares (40,500 acres) and native pastures half that much. Haymaking remained the most essential enterprise, since each head of cattle—7,200 in all—required 1.2 metric tons of hay for winter feed and the 3,600 horses also received some hay near the end of the winter season. About 70 percent of the hay was cut in the old way, by hand with scythes, and the remainder by the *sovkhoz's* five mowers. Djarkhan possessed one of these machines, but only 14 of the state farm's 120 tractors and 4 of its 60 trucks.[51] Some hay came from meadows as far distant from Toybokhoy as 150 kilometers (93 miles). Hauling hay from distant meadows to the villages was a burdensome winter activity that raised questions about the wisdom of having clustered the population in a few large settlements.

The population of Toybokhoyskiy totaled 4,600, living in 1,700 households, geographer Wein reported. Djarkhan was home to about 15 percent of these people, but possessed only 10 percent of the state farm's machines. Hard feelings and rivalry between Djarkhan and Toybokhoy villages, if not already intense, would soon escalate in post-Soviet times.

From Toybokhoyskiy in 1989 a rather impressive volume of produce flowed to the state each year. Included were 3,350 metric tons of milk, 710 of beef, and 250 of horseflesh. State-owned agribusiness obviously still functioned. We have been unable to calculate the true monetary value of this produce and do not know how many rubles went to the *sovkhoz* from the state as wages and subsidies. What we can say is that the Soviet government spent *far* more on Toybokhoyskiy than it received in value of produce. The state farm was a big money-losing enterprise.

We would also need to calculate what it would have cost the state to ship the milk and meat needed in places like Mirny, had Toybokhoyskiy not existed, in order to calculate the cost-effectiveness of the state farm. Due to the paucity of data, such calculations are impossible. Only an economist would attempt them with a straight face, and we are mere geographers. Maybe the enterprise made economic sense after all, particularly if considered in the light of Mirny's diamond profits.

## FOLK LIFE IN SOVIET DJARKHAN

Given the far-reaching transformation of life brought to Oybon's shore by collectivization, by *kolkhoz* and *sovkhoz*, how did Yakut folkways fare in the new order? Did Russification, both subtle and overt, undermine Yakut ethnicity in the *alases*? Did joining the modern world and attaining prosperity destroy the traditional culture? In much of the Soviet Union, socialism greatly eroded folk cultures.[52] Djarkhan would not go untouched.

Without question, the greatest impact occurred in shamanism and traditional cosmology, already under attack in czarist times. An edict issued in 1924 outlawed shamanism, though the practice lingered for decades in Djarkhan. A shaman was summoned to the deathbed of Bella's grandmother in 1945, and the Vilyui Bend had been known for centuries as a stronghold of such activity. Villagers recall that some shamanism survived into the 1950s, but after that it essentially disappeared.[53]

Still, traditional Yakut cosmology and superstition continued to surface in everyday life, usually in innocuous ways. For example, mothers rarely praised their children, for fear of making the spirits envious. Bella's mother Olga criticized her daughter's looks from time to time, wishing aloud that her eyes were larger or that she were just a bit taller. Bella reached twenty-five years of age before Olga told her that in fact she was very beautiful, explaining that mothers criticize in order to protect.

Russian Orthodox Christianity, never more than superficial in the Vilyui Bend *alases*, also waned under the barrage of Soviet atheism. Still, the double-barred Orthodox cross continued to compete with the red star, hammer, and scythe of Communism on grave markers in Djarkhan's cemeteries (Fig. 4.13).

Many other folk customs and practices survived. The hunters of Djarkhan continued to give a bit of food and vodka to their campfire to assure success. People still uttered the ritualistic word *huk* before eating bear meat, as an appeasement to the spirits for killing the animal. Most houses still faced east, obeying the ancient geomancy, even if that meant turning the backside to the village streets. Folk architecture found its way abundantly into the Djarkhan landscape, as we have seen, and folk costumes survived for festival occasions (Fig. 4.14).

The great Yakut midsummer's festival, Ysyakh, was forbidden in Stalin's time but vigorously revived in the more liberal Soviet rule of later decades. Authorities even allowed the establishment of a festival park on the edge of the forest north of the Kelteghey Alas. In part, though, this was to control the event, confining it to a specific place and date, to minimize the loss of work time.[54]

Traditional folk crafts also survived. The fame of the Vilyui Bend Yakuts as woodworkers and cabinetmakers continued in, for example, the workshop of Danila Tikhonov. If his furniture, today crowded into the log house in Djarkhan, could be transported to the antique shops of Europe or the United States, it would fetch thousands of dollars. Bella still

Figure 4.13. *The Orthodox Christian cross competes with the hammer, sickle, and red star of Communism in the main Djarkhan graveyard. (Photograph by Bella Bychkova Jordan, 1996.)*

remembers the smell of wood shavings in Danila's workshop and his greeting, "Oh, my child," when she appeared at the threshold to watch him at work.

The ancient hunting culture complex also survived, though not without being beneficially modernized. The advent of Communist rule brought the end of overhunting of fur-bearing animals, the reintroduction of sables to many areas where they had been extinct, the

Figure 4.14. *A birthday celebration during the late Soviet era brings forth Yakut folk dress. Tanya Tikhonova, second from right, was fifty years old this day. Oybon Lake is seen in the background. (Photograph from the Tikhonov family collection, Djarkhan, 1991.)*

annulment of Yakut debts to fur merchants, and the establishment of collective hunting-trapping stations. These stations served to instruct designated village hunters and trappers in new, conservation-based techniques, and supplied them with small-caliber rifles, ammunition, steel traps, tents, and stoves.[55] Djarkhan's collective farm leaders appointed several villagers as the official hunters and trappers. Certain other members of the collective had the task of supplying the hunter camps with necessities and transporting the catch back to the village. This became one reliable, if modest source of income for Soviet Djarkhan.

The Sakhalar of Djarkhan never forgot these folkways, but more than that, all through the Soviet times, they never forgot who they were. Many enthusiastically embraced Marxism-Leninism, but without becoming Russians. Indeed, Djarkhan produced an astounding number of high Communist Party officials, some of whom still had a bone or two to pick with the new American son-in-law in 1997. Through all this transition, it never occurred to them that being a Yakut was in any way compromised by being a Communist. *Russian* retained its older meaning in Djarkhan—roughly, "son-in-law." Communism proved as ineffective as the Orthodox Church, vodka, or Slavic tongue in destroying Yakut identity.

It was in this condition, then, that Djarkhan's villagers greeted post-Soviet times, and yet another series of wrenching changes thrust upon them from far away. They entered the brave new epoch as proprietors of a shaky agribusiness, as a modern people who enjoyed a relatively good standard of living and considerable freedom while displaying a toughness of spirit and enthusiasm for life. By world standards, they were healthy, wealthy, and wise. Above all, they entered the new age as Sakhalar.

# 5 · POST-SOVIET DJARKHAN

Profound change came to Russia in the wake of political liberalization, the disintegration of the Soviet Union, and the collapse of Communism. These changes reached remote Djarkhan with startling speed, transforming rural life in less than a decade. The result has been a modified land-use system, changed living standards, a restructured settlement morphology, an altered demography, and a revised socioeconomic order. Change continues and even intensifies at present, with no new equilibrium yet established. Only the collectivization of the 1930s, which created Djarkhan, brought comparable upheaval and change.

## DEMOGRAPHIC CHANGE

Djarkhan well represents post-Soviet Russia's demographic instability. Its population has fluctuated disconcertingly since 1991 (Table 5.1). Initially, the village grew, as it absorbed contingents of native pensioners and jobless persons from the cities of the Sakha Republic. Between 1991 and 1993 Djarkhan increased from 671 to 721 inhabitants, reaching its largest size in history. Then the migration flow reversed, and by 1997 the village's population was only 635, a decline of 12 percent in only four years and 5.4 percent just since 1996. Since then the population has stabilized; Djarkhan had 639 inhabitants at century's end.[1]

Clearly, Djarkhan has begun to experience, if belatedly, the net emigration from rural areas that has characterized Sakha-Yakutia for over a decade. In the Republic as a whole, rural areas experienced a net loss of 115 persons per 10,000 population in the period 1989 to 1995, and rural emigration has intensified in subsequent years. The population of Suntar ulus remained stable at about 27,000 between 1991 and 1998, but this masked a modest local migration from the villages to the county seat, Suntar. By 1997, about ten empty dwellings could be detected in Djarkhan. Births no longer outnumber deaths in the village, and the vigorous natural increase evident as recently as 1994 has ended. Births fell from a high of twenty-one in 1993 to only seven by 1995 and six in 1999.[2]

It is younger people who leave, seeking economic opportunity in cities such as Mirny and Yakutsk. Young women emigrate in greater numbers than men. The number of weddings fell from twelve in 1992 to only one in 1995 and two in 1998. As a consequence, Djarkhan's population is increasingly elderly (Fig. 5.1). Pensioners, including all men over the age of fifty-five and women over fifty, grew in number from 105 in 1988 to 163 in 1999.[3]

Still, as described in chapter 2, the village remains full of children. School enrollment stood at 158 in 1999, with an additional 85 preschoolers, a total of 243, or 38 percent of Djarkhan's population. This represents a legacy of very high birth rates in the 1980s. Djarkhan well reflected Sakha's high rural total fertility rate (TFR) (calculated as the average number of children women bear during their lifetime) of 2.713 in 1989. The rural TFR for the republic collapsed to 2.110 by 1994, then rebounded to 2.797 in 1996. Actual population decline began in most of rural Sakha in 1995, due to emigration.[4]

### Table 5.1 Population of Post-Soviet Djarkhan

| Year | Total Population | Births | Deaths | Net Migration |
|------|------------------|--------|--------|---------------|
| 1991 | 671 | 17 | 3 | −13 |
| 1992 | 677 | 18 | 5 | −7 |
| 1993 | 721 | 21 | 3 | +26 |
| 1994 | 670 | 20 | 12 | −59 |
| 1995 | 688 | 7 | 2 | +13 |
| 1996 | 653 | ? | ? | ? |
| 1997 | 635 | ? | ? | ? |
| 1999 | 639 | 6 | 6 | ? |

*Source:* "Demograficheskiye dannye" 1984–99.

## AGRICULTURAL CHANGE

The demographic turmoil in Djarkhan and all of rural Sakha-Yakutia is rooted mainly in agrarian change, including the abolition of the state farm system, as required by recent Russian laws, and the shift to a market economy. The Law of the Peasant Farm in 1990 encouraged privately owned agricultural enterprises, and Boris Yeltsin's 1991 decree demanded that all farmland be converted within several years to some form of peasant ownership. A *sovkhoz* such as Toybokhoyskiy, encompassing Djarkhan, could become privately owned cooperatives, joint-stock companies, partnership associations of separate peasant farms, or fully independent individual family enterprises. All government ownership of state farms ended. By January 1994, in the Sakha Republic as a whole, 97 percent of the *sovkhozy* and *kolkhozy* had been restructured to end state ownership and control.[5]

Djarkhan's villagers stoically participated in these events. Toybokhoyskiy State Farm disbanded in 1993, and each constituent village went its own way. The livestock that had belonged to the state farm was divided among the different villages, and the people of Djarkhan resented the farmers of Toybokhoy village, who, they claim, seized more than their fair share in the breakup. By contrast, the drawing of borders between the various villages went amicably. Surveyors were still at work delimiting Djarkhan's lands in 1997, but it was clear that the village would receive essentially its traditional territory, which stretches largely northwestward from the settlement (Map 2.2).[6]

A locally owned village cooperative at once replaced the state farm in Djarkhan, retaining much of the local administrative structure of the deposed system. Initially, 135 villagers joined the cooperative, which assumed ownership of most of the machinery, livestock, and milk-processing facilities that had belonged to the local division of the Soviet state farm. The cooperative also retained the traditional specialization in bovine dairy products. The government provided 70 percent of the salaries for the cooperative.[7]

The Djarkhan cooperative failed within a few years, in part because government subsidies decreased. In late Soviet times, the state farm had received not only regular agricultural subsidies from the national government, but also extra funds because of its location in agriculturally marginal lands. By contrast, Djarkhan's post-Soviet subsidies, which come from the Republic, do not exceed those given to villages in the environs of Yakutsk, which

Figure 5.1. *Demographic shifts threaten to convert Djarkhan into a village of the elderly. (Photograph by Terry G. Jordan-Bychkov, 1997.)*

enjoy good access to market. The post-Soviet subsidies, amounting to thirty-six cents per kilo of milk, proved inadequate to sustain commercial dairying. Moreover, the milk subsidy payments often failed to reach Djarkhan.[8]

Another of the problems the cooperative faced was lack of sufficient milk-processing capability and the absence of cold storage facilities. In July weather, the peak of the milking season, preserving milk became impossible. When we interviewed the cooperative leader in 1996, he complained that much of the milk spoiled every day.[9] The poor condition of the cooperative dairy was clearly evident in that year at the summer herding camp called Tyattir, a settlement of three log dwellings built around a courtyard. A large, decaying shed nearby housed two lethargic attendants using machines to milk thirty cows. The milk had to be transported daily to the processing plant in Djarkhan, about 5 kilometers (3 miles) away, but only horse-drawn wagons were available for the purpose. The modern age slipped away at Tyattir. It had been abandoned by 1997.

Earlier in the 1990s, the Swedish government built a milk-processing factory at Krestyakh, west of Djarkhan on the Vilyui River, to convert milk into a durable fluid in cardboard containers. Djarkhan's milk could conceivably have reached this factory, but the workers at Krestyakh proved unable to cope with the sophisticated machinery and technology. The plant closed, and with it probably any hope for commercial dairying in the Vilyui Bend region.[10]

Similarly, local beef production could not be made competitive in the market economy. Beef subsidies also proved inadequate and unreliable. The cost to produce a kilogram of beef in the Djarkhan cooperative in 1996 was about $4.15, while beef subsidies amounted to only thirty-four cents per kilogram and the going price of beef at stores in the Republic could not by law exceed $1.15 per kilogram. Djarkhan's remote location also contributed to the failure in marketing beef, just as it had in the demise of commercial dairying. The opening in 1997 of a beef-processing plant in Toybokhoy came too late to rescue Djarkhan's commercial meat production. In that same year the cooperative dispersed its sixty remaining cattle to private ownership among its members and went completely out of the milk and beef businesses.[11]

Part of the cooperative's difficulties also stemmed from the steady withdrawal of the more ambitious and diligent workers, who became frustrated with the inability of the leadership and members to adjust to new conditions. Too much of the old Soviet mentality persisted in the cooperative, combined with a lack of entrepreneurial expertise. Membership fell to forty-two by 1996, and to thirty by 1997, leaving behind mainly a hardcore residue of "slackers." Those who withdrew took with them much of the livestock, as well as the right to use certain parcels of land.[12]

The rump cooperative shifted entirely to horseflesh production, based on a herd that numbered 549 in 1997, down by 244, or 28 percent, from the 1991 state farm herd (Fig. 5.2). Because the hardy Yakutian horses require little winter feed, foraging for themselves in the coldest conditions, the cooperative also reduced hay production. The members did not even selectively castrate stallions, leaving breeding to Darwinian dictates. Despite the labor-extensive nature of the restructured enterprise, horse raising proved economically marginal. Dietary preferences differ ethnically, and horsemeat could only be marketed among Sakhalar. The large, dominantly Russian mining city of Mirny, west of Djarkhan, offered no outlet. Only the Yakut-populated administrative seat, Suntar, served as a market. However, the dealers there who contracted for Djarkhan's horsemeat often failed to pay after a delivery. Another factor that worked to the disadvantage of the cooperative was that horseflesh production is seasonal. In the absence of a meat-processing and storage plant, villagers had to wait until early November, when the temperatures fall below freezing, to start operations at the village's new slaughter shed (Fig. 5.3). This period extends until mid-March.[13]

These problems led to bankruptcy. As of mid-1996, the cooperative's debts, owed mainly to a bank in Suntar, stood at about $167,000, including $53,000 previously spent on

Figure 5.2. *The Djarkhan cooperative's unruly herd of open-range horses, raised for their meat, at large in the area of the old state farm at the eastern end of the village. (Photograph by Terry G. Jordan-Bychkov, 1997.)*

Figure 5.3. *The cooperative's new slaughter shed for horses, a facility that lacks refrigeration and can operate only in winter. (Photograph by Terry G. Jordan-Bychkov, 1997.)*

Figure 5.4. *One of the collapsed barns of the defunct* sovkhoz *at Djarkhan, a symbol of the events that have swept the village, republic, and country. (Photograph by Terry G. Jordan-Bychkov, 1997.)*

cattle feed. At that same time, the cooperative had $40,000 in uncollected debts owed to it, mainly by meat dealers, leaving an operating deficit of about $127,000, which can never be recovered. By 1997, the debts had mounted even more. In addition, the cooperative owed hundreds of thousands of dollars to Sakha's government to repay long-term loans. The situation in Djarkhan was typical for Sakha, where extremely high levels of debt, among the highest in all of Russia, characterize socialized farming units.[14] The Russian federal budget offers no chance for relief, because it recently stipulated a 39 percent cut in allocations for agriculture.[15] All commercial marketing of produce has ceased at Djarkhan, and the horse herd dwindled to 394 by 1999, by then apparently entirely in private ownership.

Striking visual evidence of the demise of both the state farm and the cooperative can be found in the utter ruin of the huge, elongated barns that once dominated the state farm complex in the eastern end of Djarkhan (Fig. 5.4). These barns housed the dairy herds during the long winter and contained storage for the huge amounts of hay required to carry the cattle through the seven-month winter. Today, the ruins cast a depressing pall of decay over the entire settlement. Also fallen into ruin are many kilometers of the wooden rail fences that formerly enclosed meadows and fields. No grains are raised in Djarkhan today, and the remaining small herds of dairy cows pasture in the *alases* nearest the village where no hay is cut.

Similarly, Djarkhan's farm machinery deteriorated. In 1988 the villagers had fourteen tractors, four large trucks, and six mowers, but difficulty obtaining replacement parts, coupled with high prices for fuel, caused a decline in the use of machinery. In 1997 the village possessed only four remaining tractors, and the cooperative could not afford a new motor for one of them, though two years later the number of tractors had mysteriously risen to eleven. In the village streets traditional horse-drawn wagons now rival the tractor. All cutting of hay is once again done by hand.[16]

Figure 5.5. *Independent peasant farmer Vladimir Kondratiev—prototype or eccentric? (Photograph by Bella Bychkova Jordan, 1996.)*

## PRIVATE FARMS

A few of those who withdrew from the cooperative established independent peasant farms, as allowed under post-Soviet legislation. In the Sakha Republic, more than 2,700 such farms had been established by the end of 1993, averaging forty-two hectares in size. Only four of those independent peasant farms exist in Djarkhan today.[17] Of these, the most successful is the Vladimir Kondratiev farm, operated by a man in his early sixties who formerly operated the village store (Fig. 5.5). Kondratiev left the cooperative in 1993 and claimed exclusive use of a piece of good-quality grassland some distance northeast of the village at an *alas* called Alexei-Maara near Chookar. He took an interest-free government loan for the purchase of a tractor and other needed items, and now operates a livestock farm with fifty cattle, including twenty milk cows. Kondratiev produces a substantial hay crop to feed his herd. He markets beef largely through barter at Suntar. The Republic's government owes him subsidies but has so far not paid. Even so, the farm supports twenty members of the extended Kondratiev family, which includes ten adults. The family lives on the farm

Figure 5.6. *Kondratiev farmstead, in an* alas *northeast of Djarkhan. It is a throwback to the Yakut hamlets of prerevolutionary times. (Photograph by Bella Bychkova Jordan, 1996.)*

year-round in several large log houses, avoids purchasing items at the village store, and produces much of its own food. Their settlement resembles a prerevolutionary Yakut hamlet, undoing the work of the Soviet state altogether (Fig. 5.6). The chances for long-term success remain in question, though according to official statistics only 3.5 percent of peasant farms in Sakha failed in the period 1992 to 1993. In any case, Kondratiev is an old man by local standards, having already surpassed the average male lifespan and no similarly motivated heir is apparent.[18]

A second private farm, named Development and also established in 1993, is operated by the interrelated Potapov and Simyonov families. They claimed rights to lands in the Soppon Alas, at Kuosan, east of Djarkhan, site of the pre-Soviet hamlet where their ancestors once lived. This extended family, consisting of two households, built traditional palisaded Yakut dwellings, which they recently insulated for year-round residence, as well as barns and sheds. They, too, specialize in cattle raising.[19] Their enterprise is guarded by vicious dogs, making any approach to the farmstead hazardous.

These private farmers still do not own the land they work. Land ownership is now vested in the village, and the villagers hear much about private land titles as a future or even imminent reform, but in fact nothing has actually happened. The Kondratievs, Potapovs, and Simyonovs have merely obtained the right from village authorities to use certain lands once possessed by their ancestors, and they must pay rent. Nobody in Djarkhan challenges their right. Remarkably, knowledge concerning who owned which *alases* survived six decades of Soviet control, from collectivization in the 1930s to the present day.

## SUBSISTENCE

The remaining, far larger part of Djarkhan's agricultural population has reverted to part-time subsistence farming. By 1997, these villagers owned most of the local cattle, which totaled at least 897, a surprising increase of 69 percent in numbers since 1991.

At century's end, the village census counted 888 cattle, including 324 milk cows, all of which were privately owned. Most families possess several milk cows, continuing a tradition that survived intact through Soviet times. In summer the cows drift largely without supervision from pastures near the village during daytime back to their penned calves in the village at night, where dung fires are lit to protect them from insect swarms. Hay cut from surrounding meadows provides winter fodder, and some families reside during the haying season in traditional camps at a distance from the village. In the autumn many of the fattened cattle are slaughtered for beef. During the cold months, from September to April, the remaining cows, heifers, bulls, and calves are housed in small barns of traditional design, located on each farmstead. Djarkhan's 1997 hay crop was ruined by unusually heavy rains, necessitating a massive import of hay funded by the Republic.

These villagers also owned at least 394 horses in 1999, some of which are work animals, after the cooperative's horse herd was distributed to private ownership. Because privately held livestock are taxed, the villagers underreport their numbers, so the actual totals may be as much as 40 percent higher than reported in the annual censuses. Poultry and swine are also found in some farmsteads. Rabbit raising on a modest scale began in Djarkhan in 1994, but they, too, are slaughtered before cold weather sets in. The 1999 census counted 273 chickens and 66 rabbits in Djarkhan.[20]

Kitchen gardens, both in the open air and in greenhouses, form another component of subsistence farming in Djarkhan, yielding mainly potatoes, cucumbers, tomatoes, and radishes. Cumulatively, these gardens include thirteen hectares (thirty-two acres) of land.

Together, all such private subsistence enterprises provide a substantial part of Djarkhan's food supply. In fact, twelve of these farmers, all of whom had withdrawn from the village cooperative and represented the harder-working, more ambitious element, formed their own, rival cooperative. By forming this cooperative, they were able to acquire subsidies and equipment they could not claim as individuals. Still, they do not market their produce —largely beef, milk, and butter—outside the village.[21]

The village does not survive on subsistence farming alone. Djarkhan today relies heavily on nonagricultural government funds, including wages and pensions. In 1997, about $15,000 per month was paid to all of the people of Djarkhan together in the form of pensions and welfare stipends. An additional $11,700 was due monthly as salaries for the village's 114 service-sector employees, but this money usually arrives late. By the end of 1998, the cumulative monthly salaries for the total population had fallen to the equivalent of about $4,200, though the decline may have more to do with the volatile ruble-dollar exchange rate than with real monetary value. Altogether, 313 of the village's residents, almost precisely half of the total population, receive government payments. These funds allow the villagers to survive.[22]

The agricultural decline of Djarkhan in post-Soviet times generally reflects what is happening in Sakha at large. Between 1989 and 1996, the republic's grain production dropped from 35,000 to 7,000 metric tons, while dairy cows declined in number by 12 percent, swine by 41 percent, commercial milk production by 33 percent, and potato harvests by 8 percent. Meat production held steady, but that probably reflects a slaughter of livestock to reduce herd size. But even with these declines in production, the republic is faring far better agriculturally than the remainder of the Russian Far East. Sakha's diamond wealth has allowed it to replace, at least in part, the agricultural subsidies that used to come from the government in Moscow. At the same time, everyone recognized that any increase in food production in the republic, which is and always has been food deficient, would have to be far more heavily subsidized.[23]

## LIVING STANDARD

The economic troubles of the village have been accompanied by changes in the standard of living, though by no means has the trend been universally downward. One of the best indices is provided by health standards. The entire Sakha Republic was characterized in 1996 as having a "poor state of population health." Doctors in Suntar report that health conditions in the administrative district have deteriorated since 1990, due in part to spreading malnutrition and vitamin deficiencies. Perhaps the best index of health conditions and of living standards is the infant mortality rate—the number of babies per thousand live births not surviving to the age of one. The infant mortality rate in rural areas of the Sakha Republic rose from 21.1 per thousand in 1990 to 24.9 by 1994, but then fell to only 21.8 in 1996, suggesting a trend toward improved health conditions. Life expectancy in rural Sakha fell from 65.9 to 63.3 between 1990 and 1994, but then stabilized and rose slightly to 64.1 years by 1996. Medicines were no longer available at Djarkhan's infirmary by 1996 and had to be purchased instead in Suntar, with patients bearing the expense. A new pharmacy and infirmary, manned by one doctor and three paramedics, opened in the village in 1997. A new hospital has been established at nearby Toybokhoy. Moreover, Djarkhan's residents now have access to a medical evacuation helicopter, which can transport the sick to the larger, better-equipped hospital at Suntar.[24]

In general, however, the transport links between Djarkhan and the outside world have seriously deteriorated. The high price of aviation fuel and loss of a supporting subsidy put an end to the inexpensive weekly flights from the village to Suntar, which were so popular in Soviet times. Djarkhan's airstrip has vanished into meadowland, and the small, bush-pilot, propeller-driven airplane now stands mothballed at the Suntar airport (Fig. 5.7). Similarly, all bus service to Djarkhan recently has been terminated. To reach Suntar or even Toybokhoy today, one must own a motor vehicle or hitch a ride from someone who does. The first fifteen kilometers (nine miles) of the dirt road leading out of the village are in particularly poor condition and regularly become impassable during wet weather in the summer (Fig. 5.8). In order to live beyond the subsistence level, villages in Sakha "are totally dependent on transportation lines," which in post-Soviet times "operate under constant threat of disruption," mainly from simple deterioration.[25] Djarkhan has rarely, in its seven-decade history, been more isolated and remote than at present. It remains to be seen whether the Sakha Republic will invest some of its abundant mineral wealth in rural road infrastructure, in the absence of any such initiatives at the level of the Russian government.

Offsetting these transportation problems is the rise of motor vehicle ownership. Motorcycles, many with passenger sidecars, are the most common vehicles, numbering ninety-six in 1999, up from twenty-three in 1988. Three villagers have snowmobiles. Ownership of automobiles and jeeps increased from none in 1988 to fifteen in 1996 and twenty in 1997, though the number declined to eighteen at century's end (Fig. 5.9).[26]

As recently as 1970 electricity was still turned on only for certain periods each day, when the diesel generator operated, but today electricity is cheap and abundant in

Figure 5.7. *Once this small Aeroflot bush plane flew between Djarkhan's grassy airfield and the district seat of Suntar, but no more. Today it sits mothballed beside the dirt airstrip at Suntar, a victim of budgetary cuts and fuel shortages. (Photograph by Terry G. Jordan-Bychkov, 1997.)*

Figure 5.8. *The dirt track leading from Djarkhan to Usun-Kyuel is the village's only link to the outside world. (Photograph by Terry G. Jordan-Bychkov, 1997.)*

Figure 5.9. *The New Russia has been good to this Djarkhan man: he owns not only this jeep but also the two-story house shown in Figure 5.12.*

Djarkhan, thanks to a large hydroelectric plant on the Vilyui River near Mirny. Electrical appliances such as television, radios, washing machines, and refrigerators are common, and Djarkhan receives television signals from two different towers. Satellite dishes even grace a few local homes, and some people have telephones with long-distance connections. Video cameras have become a village fad, and the foreign visitor at times sees two or three pointed in his direction. The Soviet-era practice of showing movies at the community hall was discontinued, but it is not viewed as a hardship, given the spread of VCRs and rental movies. Djarkhan even has its own Yakut-language radio station, which broadcasts village news and music.[27]

The village store provides another index of the local standard of living. Imported items such as Gerber Baby Food, Uncle Ben's Rice and "Bavaria" beer from the Netherlands could be purchased there in 1997, in addition to basic canned and dry foods, packaged fruit juices, and locally baked bread. A small selection of clothing and hardware is also available. Clerks usually ignore the new digital cash register in favor of the abacus, but clearly the store has become modernized and offers a much larger selection than it did in Soviet times. This impressive array of goods has somewhat diminished since the summer of 1998.

Djarkhan retains its excellent schools. In very late Soviet times, a large new educational complex was built, and the modern village continues to enjoy the benefits. The official school photograph for 1994 showed thirty-one employees (Fig. 5.10), and in 1999 the number of teachers stood at twenty-four. A new village council hall and community hall were also constructed in 1990. These attractive new building complexes help offset the image of decay presented by the ruined state farm barns (Fig. 5.11). A

Figure 5.10. *Djarkhan's sizable staff of teachers and other school workers. Their wages no longer arrive on time, causing hardship. (Official school photograph, 1994, from the personal collection of Aleksandra Tikhonova, who sits at the far right in the front row.)*

Figure 5.11. *Part of Djarkhan's new school complex, built at the end of the Soviet period. (Photograph by Aleksandra Tikhonova, 1997.)*

Figure 5.12. *The ultimate status symbol in post-Soviet Djarkhan and the Republic of Sakha at large: a two-story house, built of notched logs. (Photograph by Terry G. Jordan-Bychkov, 1997.)*

subsidy from the Sakha government is available to anyone building a new house, and the sound of power saws and hammers echoed through the village in the summer of 1997.[28]

Well-stocked store shelves and Western-style consumerism mask the fact that many Djarkhan residents are financially unable to make such purchases. Pensions cannot cover the rising prices of food and medicines. Wages often arrive four to six months late, causing additional problems. In 1998, for the first time, pension payments were also delayed. As in Russia at large, a minority has prospered under the new system, but most people have experienced a decline in their living standard. A class-based society is emerging, even in this remote place.[29] A small number of people have acquired disproportionate access to and control of the village's resources. The new status symbols in Djarkhan, attainable by those who have coped successfully with the post-Soviet economy, are two-story houses (Fig. 5.12) and automobiles or jeeps. The present economic crisis now threatens even those who initially prospered in the new system.

## YAKUT VILLAGE CULTURE

The increased isolation of villages like Djarkhan, combined with the collapse of pervasive central authority and planning, have prompted a revival of traditional Yakutian rural culture. The increased autonomy of the Sakha Republic further facilitates this development. The Sakha cultural revival will perhaps be modest, given the many decades during which Yakut folkways declined. Shamanism, for example, probably has little chance to come

Figure 5.13. *Three members of Djarkhan's extended Tikhonov family display their clan chieftain's ceremonial sash and, with it, pride in their family. Such artifacts and pride were suppressed in Soviet times and have now reemerged. From left to right are Olga Tikhonova, Ksenia Ammosova, and Aida Petrova. Bella's great-grandfather was clan chief and wore this sash. (Photograph by Terry G. Jordan-Bychkov, 1997.)*

back in force, though a few shamanistic traditions survived the Soviet period here and there in rural Sakha, and at least five well-known shamans have surfaced in the republic lately. A revival of folk-medicinal practices is occurring, especially along the Vilyui. In Djarkhan, one woman healer, a "white," or benign, shaman, plies this trade today.[30]

Interest in genealogy and pride in one's ancestry, suppressed in the Soviet era, have revived in post-Soviet times. Djarkhan's extended Tikhonov family provides a good example. Members do not hesitate to tell outsiders that "ours was once a rich family," and a venerable tricolor Tikhonov clan chieftain's sash, hidden for seven decades, is once again displayed with pride (Fig. 5.13). The family claims descent from a runaway Russian exile, Seluyan Tikhonov, who married a local Yakut woman in the late seventeenth century, and started the clan. A shrine commemorating the family's origin was recently erected near a small grove outside the village (Fig. 5.14). Every summer the extended family gathers there for a celebration.[31]

The greatest Yakut folk festival, the midsummer's Ysyakh, is also experiencing a revival. Soviet authorities had restricted the festival to a few days and obliged every village to hold the event on the same week in an attempt to diminish the overt ethnicity of Ysyakh and the substantial inroads it made on the rural work schedule. Now the dates have been staggered, allowing itinerant musicians and athletes to perform at multiple celebrations, in the ancient manner. Celebrants, too, can now attend more than one Ysyakh each summer.

Figure 5.14. *Private family shrine commemorating the ancestor of Djarkhan's Tikhonov family, a runaway Russian exile, Seluyan Tikhonov, who married a Yakut woman and settled near Lakes Oybon and Ebe in the late 1600s. The family gathers here for midsummer new year celebrations. This remarkable genealogy survived in oral tradition, even through Soviet times, and now enjoys a revival. (Photograph by Terry G. Jordan-Bychkov, 1997.)*

Figure 5.15. *Vasily Tikhonov sharpens his scythe in the far haymeadows beyond Lake Borullo. Such traditional methods never completely disappeared and many are now experiencing a revival. Vasily has seen a bit of the world, having served with the Soviet military in Cuba in the 1960s. (Photograph by Terry G. Jordan-Bychkov, 1997.)*

Perhaps the most interesting revival of the traditional Yakut way of life is the previously mentioned return of a few private farmers to their ancestral *alases.* The Kondratievs, Potapovs, and Simyonovs are, in effect, attempting to reestablish the prerevolutionary settlement fabric of scattered hamlets. Given the scattered distribution of *alases,* this traditional settlement pattern is a more efficient one, reducing travel distance and time, but it remains to be seen how many of the local Sakhalar are willing or able to give up the amenities of village life (Map 2.1). Revival of tradition is also seen in the trend back to hand tools and horse-drawn vehicles (Fig. 5.15). These reversions to the old ways stand in stark contrast to the proliferation of video cameras, VCRs, and refrigerators found in the villages today.

## TIME OF FLUX

As the twentieth century ended, a century so full of profound change, a century that brought the outside world to the shores of Lake Oybon and revolutionized life there, Djarkhan's villagers faced an uncertain and unknowable future. Who, after all, would have predicted a decade ago the transformation of life that has already occurred here?

Everything remains in flux. A new stability, a "post-post-Soviet" order, has yet to reveal itself in any fixed manifestation. Uncertainty is the only certainty, a condition stressful even for a stoic people whose capacity to endure and survive suffering surpasses Western comprehension. Forces far beyond the control of the villagers of Djarkhan will, as usual, determine the fate of the community. We can only hazard educated guesses concerning twenty-first-century Djarkhan, but such an exercise seems essential.

# 6 · DO NOT VANISH, MY VILLAGE

Djarkhan, in its present episode of instability and restructuring, faces a "chaotic and unknown future," in common with many other Siberian rural places.[1] The trends today are diverse and in some measure run counter to one another. We can view the situation in Djarkhan at the dawn of a new century and plausibly suggest several very different outcomes, ranging from abandonment to village viability.

Predicting the future is a hazardous undertaking, particularly in times of rapid change, and while social scientists have an abysmal prognosticative record, we feel that we know this place and people well enough to make some educated guesses concerning Djarkhan —and the 250 other farm villages similar to it in Sakha—in the twenty-first century.[2] All too rarely do geographers use their intimate knowledge of places for predictive purposes, leaving the field to economists and historians, who rarely venture away from their archives and number crunching to inspect the real world at the level of community and province. Whatever our sins of omission, this is not among them.

We make only one disclaimer concerning our predictions. They assume the continuity of the Russian state, its rule over Siberia, and its domestic tranquility, none of which can be regarded as certain. Everything could descend into chaos, though we think that unlikely.

## ABANDONMENT?

Assuming such continuity, three future scenarios seem possible for isolated villages in the marginal lands of Russia. One of these is clearly *abandonment*.[3] Today in some parts of Siberia, "Villages dissolve into ghost towns of the elderly and immobile," and even along the Lena River, in the very heart of Sakha-Yakutia, recently deserted settlements can be seen.[4] Large sections of rural Russia could become a "demographic desert."[5] The judgment of history could well be that Djarkhan, a Soviet creation, did not long survive the demise of the system that gave it birth.

The best and brightest young adults continue to leave Djarkhan and other villages. Bella's mother Olga perhaps unwittingly set this trend in motion four decades ago when, against all odds, she left to begin a distinguished career in medicine, becoming the most famous plastic oral surgeon in Sakha-Yakutia. The village has produced a surprisingly large number of other accomplished people.[6] These emigrants not only take their talents away from the village, but also leave behind an agricultural system that cannot survive unless it is heavily subsidized, a system that has in fact already collapsed at the level of commercial farming.

Some high governmental officials in Sakha-Yakutia favor future support for only those farm villages situated near the capital, Yakutsk, in the three great, broad, grassy riverine valleys—Erkyani, Tooymaada, and Anseli—strung like pearls along the middle Lena. These valleys enjoy good access to market, especially the former two, which are linked to the capital by paved highways. Vitaly P. Artamonov, Sakha's minister of foreign relations (at the time of our interview), who grew up, as most Yakuts did, in a farm village, favors abandonment of all agricultural enterprises in the Republic, drawing the entire rural population into the cities and towns, rather than having "my people live as in the times of Ghengis Kahn!"[7] Obviously, he is not very nostalgic about his rural youth. To another interviewer Artamonov said the Sakha government should bring the Even reindeer herders closer to Yakutsk, so they "could abandon this Stone Age life."[8]

Innokentiy Pakhomov, the influential leader of the Sakha Republic's Committee for Land Reform (and born in Djarkhan), is deeply attached to his natal village. The author of a pamphlet outlining Djarkhan's history, he concedes that abandonment remains a possibility, though he remains optimistic that it won't happen.[9] Minister Pakhomov, of course, provides another example of the brain-drain that afflicts and endangers the village. Arkady Nikiforovich Ivanov, head of the Djarkhan Village Council —*not* a native of the place—is a sensitive, intelligent man not afraid to speak his mind. He is pessimistic about the future. Djarkhan will be abandoned within ten to twenty-five years, he says, unless economic conditions improve and some employment base for the village can be developed. Commercial agriculture, he feels, cannot be viable. Ivanov knows that Djarkhan's chief natural resource is the high-quality and abundant grasslands, which are best suited for the very agricultural enterprise that can never be commercially viable. In any case, the grassland resources lie scattered about the village lands, a pattern better suited to multiple hamlets than a single, sizable village (Map 2.1). Djarkhan's very clustering—concentrating over six hundred people in one remote place —requires, will require, and has always required substantial governmental subsidies. A sadness tinges Ivanov's voice and mannerisms as he talks about the future.[10]

One might imagine that fur trapping in the extensive village lands, stretching north-westward from Djarkhan, could provide a viable industrial base. Not so. Large commercial fur farms in northern Sakha already flood the market with an oversupply of pelts, and these furs from the colder areas are of higher quality.[11] Council leader Ivanov suggested enlarging to commercial scale Djarkhan's modest lumber mill, which today supplies only the village. Good-quality timber grows abundantly in the forests around Djarkhan. However, nearby Toybokhoy already has a commercial sawmill and better road connections. In any case, a much larger sawmill recently failed in the *ulus* seat of Suntar, putting many workers on the unemployment list.[12]

All of these factors seem to presage abandonment. In truth, village abandonment has been a well-established trend in Russia since Soviet times. A 1974 decree ordered the "liquidation of unpromising villages," but in fact the process was decades older than that.[13] Indeed, as we have seen, Djarkhan owes its very creation and subsequent growth largely to settlement consolidation. Recall that the 160 inhabitants of Kuosan, a village seven kilometers to the east, were relocated to Djarkhan between 1966 and 1980. Villages died in many parts of Russia in late Soviet times. Much more recently, the federal government's failure to supply adequate winter provisions in the autumn of 1998 led to a proposal to abandon, at least temporarily, many small, remote settlements in Siberia. While Djarkhan was not among those villages, a continued and deepened crisis in Russia might logistically endanger our village.[14] The failure of commercial agriculture strongly suggests that Djarkhan, in its turn, has now also become an "unpromising" village. While some reputed experts speak of "sustainable development" in the Russian Arctic lands, Djarkhan and many other villages face a more basic task: achieving "sustainable habitation."[15] One wonders whether the words *future* and *village* combined in the titles of scholarly articles about contemporary rural Russia are not incongruous when applied to the marginal lands.[16]

Quite conceivably, then, the population of Djarkhan and neighboring villages such as Usun-Kyuel and Mar-Kyuel might be relocated south to Toybokhoy on the national route, or to Suntar, the *ulus* seat. However, neither of those places is thriving, and a testy rivalry exists between Djarkhan and Toybokhoy. It would be a bitter pill, indeed, for our villagers to be obliged to move there. Suntar suffers from severe postindustrial recession and has been labeled "economically unprogressive" by a high government official, who went so far as to say the town may have "little future."[17]

Abandonment is the easy and perhaps logical prediction to make for Djarkhan and her sister villages. Undoubtedly, it is the prediction that cloistered economists would make. To cultural geographers, though, the issue does not seem so simple. For one thing, exactly where would the departing population of Djarkhan go, and how would they earn a living when they got there? Abandonment implies a viable residential option — one that does not presently exist. But beyond these mere logistics, the cultural geographer sees that Djarkhan and villages like it are far more complicated than the "bottom line" of sterile economics. We must also consider spiritualism, mysticism, emotion, ethnicity, and attachment to place. While these factors cannot be quantified, they exist and will likely play a role in determining the future of the village.

## NEOTRADITIONALISM

The emerging body of theoretical literature on *neotraditionalism* suggests a very different scenario for the future of Djarkhan.[18] Many of the "little peoples" of Arctic Russia may respond to the collapse of the Soviet system by reverting to their traditional subsistence way of life, as if Russian culture and Marxism-Leninism had never been imposed on them.[19]

Would or could the rural Sakhalar revert to a pre-Russian way of life? Yakuts are emphatically not among the "little peoples." They number 400,000 and have thrived during the nearly four centuries of Russian rule, trading and mixing with their rulers while vigorously retaining their ethnic identity. Could they revive the ancestral "*alas* economy" of transhumant livestock herding, subsisting from their horses, cattle, hunting, fishing, and gathering?[20] Could they avoid "the cold breath of the market economy" by withdrawing from the modern world?[21] That seems highly improbable, if for no other reason than because even the rural Sakhalar have forgotten how to live that way. Ammunition has become so expensive that few can afford to hunt. And the pastoral Yakuts of old often suffered hunger and deprivation, a fate no one would wish upon a people. Nor would the Sakhalar accept such a standard of living. "Nobody can survive this way, by subsistence farming," says the government's land reform minister.[22]

In any case, to revive the old way of life would also mean abandoning Djarkhan to disperse to lakeside hamlets, where village amenities would not be available. To be sure, the independent peasant farms created recently by the Kondratiev, Potapov, and Simyonov families would seem to support the neotraditionalistic model, even down to the details of folk architecture, but it is difficult to imagine the population of Djarkhan at large choosing this path to the future. Ethnicity will surely play a role in shaping what will come, but not, we feel, in an overtly neotraditionalistic way.

Figure 6.1. *A new log house in Djarkhan, a testimony to faith in the future (and to a government subsidy). (Photograph by Bella Bychkova Jordan, 1996.)*

## TOPOPHILIA

Yakut ethnicity will more likely be demonstrated in the villagers' fierce loyalty to their home. We should never, as geographers, underestimate the love of place or, as Yi-fu Tuan called it, "topophilia."[23] He also referred to this basic human emotion as "geopiety"—the bond between people and home—and as "rootedness."[24] Similarly, E. V. Walter wrote of "the energy of places," a form of energy that does not obey the laws of thermodynamics but that can guide and influence human behavior.[25]

Read again the lyrics of the Djarkhan song in chapter 2. Conjure up once more the image of Olga returning through the polar gloom and bitter cold to give birth to her first child in the beloved native village. Look at the new dwellings under construction in Djarkhan (Fig. 6.1). The heartfelt cry "Don't vanish, my village" defies naked logic and economics.[26] It must be taken seriously by those who wish to read the future of places.

Robert Hay recently wrote of "a rooted sense of place," distinguishing between "modern" and "indigenous" geopiety.[27] The Sakhalar of Djarkhan possess a powerful indigenous and ethnic rootedness, tribal and ancestral in its force. It amounts to an ideological rootedness deriving from identification with a large community, with "insideness," as Hay put it. Now, you will ask, how can a village founded in 1932 command such emotion? To the inhabitants of Djarkhan, the year 1932 is irrelevant. In fact, nobody we talked to knew the exact year the village was founded. The point is, their ancestors have lived here, beside the waters of Oybon and Ebe, in these beautifully interlaced prairies, from time immemorial.

Djarkhan is the sole surviving local settlement; the ancient lakeside hamlets and sister socialist villages all have perished, and the full allegiance of the people now resides in this
one place. Djarkhan both assumed the name of this *alas*-rich district and focused the
potent indigenous geopiety of the local Sakhalar.

In this rootedness, ethnicity is central. Consider that when our villagers migrate to the
cities of Sakha-Yakutia, they not only make a rural-to-urban transition, but also enter the
world of Russian culture. Cities such as Yakutsk or Mirny are essentially Russian places.
Small wonder that the displaced villagers often return home, either seasonally or permanently. Their deep attachment to Djarkhan is bound up in ethnic identity and pride.

How, then, might the villagers find a way to make Djarkhan viable? All over rural Sakha-
Yakutia, this is the essential problem.[28] Cottage industries offer some hope. Souvenir manufacture was underway in the village in 1997, and the traditional Yakut talent for wood-
working and jewelry making could conceivably provide a basis for future cottage industries.
On a more prosaic level, one villager now collects manure and sells it to gardeners in the
city of Mirny. Small-scale retail capitalism has also made a beginning. One pensioner, who
spends the winter in Moscow, imports clothing to Djarkhan for sale. He is Moisey Ivanov,
the starving boy we met in chapter 4. Others bring gasoline in canisters from Suntar.
Retailing, of course, can thrive only if the villagers have money to make purchases.[29]
Moisey's clothing business has not fared well in the present crisis.[30]

Small-scale, "end-of-the-road" capitalism will help, but Djarkhan cannot survive without continued governmental subsidies, salaries, and pensions, nearly all of which now
come from the Republic rather than the Russian Federation.[31] Traditional Yakut culture
does reside in the villages, so the Republic could and should use some of its mineral
wealth to continue to subsidize the existence of places like Djarkhan, much as Norway
has. However, one high government official recently warned the rural Sakhalar, "Don't wait
for diamond money to be given to you."[32] Such subsidies are presently being provided, as
well as emergency funds. When the 1997 hay crop was largely ruined by unusually rainy
conditions, the government of Sakha distributed huge amounts of hay and fodder to
Djarkhan and other afflicted villages in the Vilyui River basin (Fig. 6.2).[33] Without that
timely assistance, the villagers would have been forced to slaughter their cattle. The subsidy for new house construction continues, though it would be better today to spend
those funds on improving road conditions.[34]

The village can also continue to depend upon the return migration of retired workers
who left Djarkhan and found employment in the cities. All of those who leave retain ownership of their village house and lot, returning seasonally for summer vacation and, in
many cases, for permanent residence upon retirement.[35] In this way, Djarkhan can survive
partly as a village of vacation *dachas*—summerhouses—and pensioners. These people
require diverse services, which provide jobs for resident storekeepers, medical personnel,
administrators, and servants. They purchase milk, meat, and other locally produced goods.
However, with the average lifespan at only sixty-three years in rural Sakha, the pensioners
are not living long enough to make Djarkhan a true retirement village.

Almost everyone in Djarkhan and in the government believes that continued operation
of the village schools is essential to the survival of the settlement.[36] Where "there is a
school, there is a future."[37] Demographic trends suggest that Djarkhan's schools in the future will have substantially smaller local enrollments. But Djarkhan, like most Yakutian villages, has friends in high places. Innokentiy Pakhomov, the Djarkhan native who heads

Figure 6.2. *The summer of 1997 was unusually rainy in Djarkhan, turning the village streets into quagmires and ruining most of the abundant hay harvest. (Photograph by Terry G. Jordan-Bychkov, 1997.)*

Sakha's Committee for Land Reform and earlier, in Soviet times, served as first secretary of the Suntar regional committee of the Communist Party, recently intervened to help his village. In 1998 Pakhomov proposed to the Suntar *ulus* Education Council that Djarkhan's excellent school and gymnasium complex become the basis of a regional boarding school for scholarship-supported student-athletes, drawn from the entire Vilyui Bend region.

Swift approval was obtained—some measure of Pakhomov's influence—and construction of a new dormitory for the complex was completed in November 1999. A month earlier, the first eighteen boarding students from other villages began the school year in Djarkhan. Suntar *ulus* provided four new teaching positions and instructional assistants to support the project, in addition to 1½ positions for launderer and janitor and six other new maintenance salaries for the school. Together, this brought 12½ new service jobs to Djarkhan, not to mention the stipend money spent in the village by the boarding students. Tragically, the new building complex burned to the ground on December 17, barely a month after completion. The people of Djarkhan, ever resilient, at once began collecting money within the village to build again.[38] The new millennium dawned bleak and ominous.

The survival of Djarkhan, then, will have to be cobbled together from diverse activities and government funds. Certain elements of the older subsistence economy, such as meat, milk, and vegetable production for local consumption, will need to survive. Hunting, gathering, and fishing will need to be pursued. If this is neotraditionalism, then that model helps us understand how Djarkhan can survive. Some segments of the service economy would have to be maintained, such as the retail facility, village administration, fuel distribution, clinic, repair shops, and the like. We can envision, for example, a shopkeeper or cottage artisan or paramedic whose family also keeps milk cows, mows hay, fishes in the lake, hunts in the forest, picks berries in season, and gardens in a small greenhouse. In fact, such families already exist in Djarkhan. To be sure, the population would be smaller than at present—perhaps three hundred or even four hundred is a reasonable goal. Sakha's minister for land reform optimistically estimates that about one-third of the republic's population will remain in the villages, a very modest decline from the situation today, when 36 percent of the republic's population lives in rural places.[39]

In this way, elements of the traditional subsistence economy could be incorporated into a diverse adaptive strategy that would also include cottage industries, government salaries, pensions, boarding students, and modest subsidies. The Djarkhan of the future would be at once ethnic, topophilic, commercial, subsistent, services oriented, subsidized, neotraditionalistic, modern, or even postindustrial.

Above all, we should not judge Djarkhan's survival chances by Western and particularly American standards. These rural Sakhalar are a tough, proud, resilient, resourceful, stoic people who have endured far worse hardships than the present ones. They believe in mutual support and have a life philosophy centered on community well-being and attachment to place. They understand the patronage system and know how to tap it.

The Sakha-Yakutia government will need to establish a firm and dependable policy subsidizing and otherwise supporting these villages, as it does piecemeal, unreliably, and haphazardly today. Above all, the people of Djarkhan, both resident and nonresident, will need to nurture the mystical bond they have with this beautiful place and continue to pass the sentiment from one generation to the next. That almost religious bond is the cement that provides the vital "sense of community."[40] If all of this happens, and we think it can, then the village will not die and the long legacy of Yakuts dwelling beside Oybon's waters will endure.

# GLOSSARY

**aga-usa** A traditional Yakut clan, including from about ten to one hundred persons; these clans had ceased to exist as units of social organization by 1900.

**alas** Yakutian word and periglacial term describing a small thermokarst depression covered with grasses and draining internally to a central lake.

**Arylakh** The name of Djarkhan village from 1932 to the late 1960s and also the former name of the lake lying just northwest of Djarkhan and of the prerevolutionary hamlet that stood on that lake; meaning "where *alases* interconnect and forest groves stand."

**Ayysyt** The Yakut goddess of fertility and plenty who delivers a soul to each newborn.

**Ayy-Toyon** The White Creator Lord in Yakut cosmology who dwells aloof in the uppermost, seventh sky in the East.

**balagan** The traditional dwelling of the Sakhalar, shaped like a truncated pyramid and consisting of walls made of beams set at a slant into the earth.

**Bayanai** Lord of the *taiga,* a spirit in Yakut cosmology who lives in the forest and must be appeased by those who enter to hunt.

**Borullo** "The place of the white-tailed eagle," a lake and *alas* not far north of Djarkhan village.

**chernozem** Russian word meaning "black earth"; fertile soils developed beneath grasslands.

**Chukchi** A native people of northeastern Siberia, closely akin to the Inuit (Eskimos), numbering about sixteen thousand.

**Djarkhan** The name of the village beside Oybon Lake, used since the late 1960s, and also the name of several subdivisions of the Suntar county since czarist times; it is derived from the name of a woman who was the presumed ancestress of the people of this village and subdivision.

**Dolgan** A small ethnic group in Sakha-Yakutia; in effect an Evenk or Even who has adopted the Yakutian language; numbering about seven thousand.

**D'Yarkhan** The clan of Sakhalar who settled the Vilyui Bend region; same as N'Urbagato; people descended from Djarkhan.

**Even** An ancient people of Sakha-Yakutia of Mongol-Manchurian origin, today numbering only seventeen or eighteen thousand and related to the Evenks.

**Evenk** An ancient people of Sakha-Yakutia and neighboring parts of Russia, numbering about thirty-one thousand today; of Mongol-Manchurian origin; called Tungus by the Russians; related to the Evens.

**geomancy** The animistic belief, found among the Sakhalar and many other peoples, that compass directions and other features of the physical geography possess good or evil spirits or qualities that must be considered when orienting and positioning dwellings, graves, doors, and the like; thus among the Sakhalar, east is good and west is bad.

**gulag**  Russian for "prison camp" or "slave-labor detention camp"; Siberia had many such places in czarist and Soviet times.

**Isikh**  See Ysyakh.

**ityan'**  A hunter's shelter, conical shaped and made of birchbark.

**Kelteghey**  A lake and *alas* near Djarkhan village, meaning "crescent-shaped."

**kolkhoz**  A Russian word meaning "collective farm"; a contraction of *kollectivnoe khozyaistvo.*

**kulak**  In precollectivization and czarist times, a wealthy landowning free peasant.

**kumyss**  Fermented mare's milk, consumed in great quantities, especially at the Yakut midsummer's (New Year's) festival.

**Kuosan**  Name of an abandoned village near Djarkhan; "Down in the hollow."

**kystyk**  Hamlet or winter hamlet, the dominant traditional Yakut rural settlement of the precollective period.

**Lena**  The great central river of Sakha-Yakutia, flowing to the Arctic Ocean; "Grandmother Lena" to the Sakhalar.

**moos ustar**  In the ancient Yakut lunar calendar, roughly April, "the month when the ice breaks."

**munkha**  A Yakut sack net used in ice fishing.

**nasleg**  Administrative subdivision, roughly "precinct" or "tribal seat," just below the level of the *ulus* (county); a Russian word, but used only in Yakutia in this meaning.

**neotraditionalism**  A model of post-Soviet ethnic tendencies in which small groups living in Arctic Russia revert by necessity to their pre-Soviet traditional ways of life; proposed by ethnographer Aleksandr Pika and geographer Boris Prokhorov.

**N'Urbagato**  See D'Yarkhan.

**N'Urbakaan**  See Djarkhan (person).

**nyucha djietya**  Yakutian for "Russian house," that is, a dwelling made of notched logs.

**Nyurgusun**  The earliest flower to bloom in the *alases; Anemone patens.*

**oblast**  Soviet and post-Soviet Russian word for a high order of nonethnic administrative district, equal in rank to a republic; equivalent to the czarist *guberniya* (roughly "governorate" or "province"); Yakutia was a *guberniya* in prerevolutionary times.

**okrug**  The level of administrative district just below the *oblast* or republic; roughly "district."

**Olonkho**  The name of the Yakutian national folkloric epic, transcribed from the oral tradition in the twentieth century.

**oot yia**  In the Yakut lunar calendar, roughly July, "the month of hay."

**örs**  In Yakutian tradition, the discontented souls of the dead, who share the Middle World with living people.

**Oybon**  "Hole cut in the ice for fishing"; the name of the lake beside which the village of Djarkhan stands and also the name of a prerevolutionary hamlet on the same site.

**periglacial**  Literally, "peripheral to glaciers"; the effects of glaciation on adjacent areas that did not lie beneath the ice.

**permafrost** The permanently frozen subsurface of the Earth, unaffected by the seasonal thaw of surface layers.

**podsol (also, _podzol_)** A boreal forest soil characterized by the downward leaching of humus and other nutrients, leaving the surface layers sterile and light-colored; adjective form is _podsolized._

**rayon (also, _raion_)** Russian word for a small administrative district, ranking below the _okrug_ and more or less the same as the Yakut _ulus;_ roughly "county"; if inhabited by an ethnic group it was called a national _rayon._

**saiylyk** A Yakutian summer herding and haying camp.

**Sakha** The Yakutian word meaning "Yakutia" and the "Yakut people," as well as "a Yakut" (singular).

**Sakhalar** The Yakutian word meaning "Yakuts" (plural).

**Sakha Republic** Same as the Republic of Sakha-Yakutia.

**Sakha-Yakutia** The correct modern name for the republic, joining the Yakutian and Russian terms to reflect the biethnic character.

**shaman** A holy person, male or female, in the traditional religion of the Sakhalar; intercedes to control and mitigate the harmful effects of evil spirits and the forces of Nature; either "white" (weak, benevolent) or "black" (strong and good or bad).

**sovkhoz** A state farm in the Soviet system, a state-owned agribusiness where the farmers are salaried employees; a contraction of the Russian _sovetskoye khozyaistvo._

**Suntar** A town on the Vilyui River and also the _ulus,_ or county, in which Djarkhan village is located; the town is the seat of the _ulus._

**suorat** A thick yogurt that is a staple of the Yakut diet.

**taiga** The boreal coniferous forests occupying a broad east-west belt across Russia and including most of Sakha-Yakutia.

**talky** A wooden press with teeth used to soften fur pelts.

**thermokarst** The melting of a top portion of the permafrost, sufficient to cause subsidence and the development of enclosed depressions such as _alases._

**thufur** Small mounds created by the repeated freezing and thawing of water trapped in small depressions.

**titik** A calf pen, where unweaned calves are kept during the day and to which the cows return voluntarily in the evening.

**Toybokhoy** A large village south of Djarkhan on the national highway; headquarters of the _sovkhoz_ that included the Djarkhan area from 1966 to 1993.

**transhumance** The seasonal migration of people with their livestock from winter quarters to summer pastures.

**tundra** The treeless expanses north of the _taiga,_ along the Arctic coast, and above the tree line in the Siberian mountain ranges; plant growth consists of sedges, rushes, mosses, lichens, grasses, and dwarf trees.

**ulus** Yakutian word for an administrative district equivalent to the Soviet _rayon,_ ranking below the _oblast_ and _okrug;_ roughly "county"; today, the highest order of nonethnic political subdivision within the Republic of Sakha-Yakutia.

**Uluu-Toyon** Deity of Yakutian cosmology residing in the third sky, in the West; potentially malevolent.

**uraha** Conical, birchbark-covered Yakut summer camp dwelling, similar to an American Indian tepee.

**Usun-Kyuel** Meaning "Long lake," Djarkhan's nearest neighbor village, to the east.

**Vilyui River** The major left-bank tributary of the Lena; "Grandfather Vilyui" to the Yakuts.

**white nights** The two-month period around the summer solstice when it does not get dark.

**Yakutia** The Russian name for Sakha.

**Yakutian (or Sakha-tyla)** The language of the Sakhalar, belonging to the Turkic division of the Altaic language family.

**Yasak** The tribute or tax paid in fur pelts, demanded by the Russians from the peoples, such as the Sakhalar, they had conquered in Siberia.

**Yot-ichchite** The spirit of the hearth fire, highly honored in the traditional religion of the Sakhalar.

**Yrae Bootur** "Singing Warrior," the eldest son of the ancestress Djarkhan; The people of the Djarkhan area claim descent from him.

**Ysyakh** The Yakut New Year celebration, held at the summer solstice; the greatest annual festival.

**Yukagirs** A paleo-Siberian ethnic group of reindeer herders, numbering about twelve hundred.

**yurt** The Yakutian word for "household" or "house;" an ancient Turkic word that means "tent."

**Yuryakh** Yakutian for a streamside grassland, a wetland where hay can be cut.

# NOTES

## 1 · SIBERIA: MYTH AND REALITY

1. Wood 1987, 36–37; Rasputin 1996, 34, 37.
2. Nansen 1914; Mostakhov 1982.
3. Hooson 1994, 129.
4. Rasputin 1996, 62, 370–72; Specter 1998, W1.
5. Hiller and Kaptilkin 1997, 17.
6. Lobanov-Rostovsky 1965, 85–86.
7. Müller 1882, 264–68.
8. Rasputin 1996, 33, 53.
9. *Random House* 1993, 1775.
10. Rasputin 1996, 36, 375.
11. Hooson 1994, 112–31; Bassin 1991.
12. Murzayev 1964; Parker 1960; Gumilev 1990.
13. Hauner 1990, 1.
14. Müller 1882, 265.
15. Mote 1998; Rasputin 1996, 376 (first quote); Hiller and Kaptilkin 1997, 17.
16. Mote 1998, 182; Balzer 1995; Argounova and Habeck 1997–98; Popova 1978,5; Lishenyuk 1995, 8, 11, 22; Azulay and Azulay 1995, 191; Mote 1998; Wein 1997.
17. *Chislennost'* 1991; Heleniak 1999, 181; Dmitriyeva 1989; *First Book* 1992, A5, B5, D5, K5; Sakha Republic 1995b; Rodgers 1990, 62; Lishenyuk 1995, 11, 24; Popova 1978, 8; Torgovkina 2000, 6; *Demograficheskiye ezhegodnik* 1996, 18, 31; 1997.
18. *Chislennost'* 1991, 1998; Heleniak 1999, 160, 172; *Demograficheskiye ezhegodnik* 1993; 1994; 1995; 1996, 28, 68, 90, 101, 112, 266, 518; 1997, 99, 110, 265; 1999; *First Book* 1992; Demko, Ioffe, and Zayonchkovskaya 1999, 141.
19. Heleniak 1999, 163; Sidorov 1984; Balzer and Vinokurova 1996, 103; Kempton 1996, 589 Torgovkina 2000, 6.
20. Mote 1998, 182; Fondahl 1997, 192; Gumilev 1990, 346; Gogolev 1993; Seroshevsky 1993; Milner-Gulland and Dejevsky 1989, 207; Pakhomov 1993; Semyonov 1944; Wixman 1984; Levin and Potapov 1964; Wein 1997; Forsyth 1992; Wieczynski 1976; Parker 1968; Bater and French 1983; Lobanov-Rostovsky 1965; Pavlov 1986.
21. Cole 1991, 589; Lewis, Rowland, and Clem 1976, 110.
22. *Istoriya Yakutskoy* 1955–63; Fondahl 1993.
23. O'Loughlin and van der Wusten 1993, 94; Dostál and Knippenberg 1979; Dwyer and Drakakis-Smith 1996; Armstrong 1967, 12.
24. Shaw 1999, 221; Wood 1987; Wood and French 1989.
25. *Rossiyskiy Statisticheskiy* 1997, 72; Vitebsky 1990; Sleptsov 1990; Harris 1993, 555, 572; Armstrong 1967, 13.
26. Mote 1998, 141, 156; Balzer 1999, 17–20; Shaw 1999, 241; Balzer 1995, 139, 142, 152–53; Fondahl 1997, 212–13; Bradshaw 1992; Chinn and Kaiser 1996; Kaiser 1995; Poelzer 1995; Shaw 1995; Clem and Craumer 1995, 74–77; "Russia's Regions" 1997, 47; Lishenyuk 1995; Kraus and Liebowitz 1996; Kempton 1996, 594–97; Lynn and Fryer 1998.
27. Strahlenberg 1738, 380; Sidorov 1984; Vitebsky 1996.
28. Drobizheva 1995, 15–23; Sheehy 1986; *Demograficheskiye ezhegodnik* 1996, 496, 502; Balzer 1995, 142–43; Fondahl 1993, 498; Balzer and Vinokurova 1996, 108–111; Klyuchevsky 1989, 107.
29. Bradshaw and Lynn 1998, 388–89; Arievich 1992, 37–38; Fondahl 1997, 213.
30. Selm 1998, 607; Stavrakis, DeBardeleben, and Black 1997, 226–27; Krasikov 1991; Balzer 1995, 149; Yegorova 1994–95, 35–37; Mote 1998, 186.

31. Lishenyuk 1995; Mote 1998, 182.

32. Fondahl 1997, 213–14; Linge 1992; Kolossov 1993; Kaiser 1994; Kaiser 1995; Hooson 1994.

33. Lydolph 1977; Suslov 1961; Popova 1978, 6; Wood 1987, 23, 25.

34. *Agroklimaticheskiye* 1973.

35. Espenshade, Hudson, and Morrison 1995, 10–11. 36. Lydolph 1990, 32, 41.

37. Koutaniemi 1985; Suslov 1961, 195.

38. Berg 1950, 31–32; *Atlas Sel'skogo* 1989; Popova 1978, 6; Wood 1987, 21–23.

39. *Atlas Sel'skogo* 1989; Prokhorov 1982, 30: 685; Popova 1978, 7.

40. Bosikov 1991; Kirikov 1983; Shubnikova 1967; Lishenyuk 1995, 22; Popova 1978, 8; Suslov 1961, 196.

41. Elovskaya and Ivanov 1989; Popova 1978, 7; Rodgers 1990, 40–41; Berg 1950, 32; Lishenyuk 1995, 22.

42. Selm 1998, 608, 614; Wines 1998, A1, A10.

43. Sakha 1995a; Sakha 1996; Lishenyuk 1995, 26.

44. Luk'yanov 1982; Fondahl 1993, 497; Kempton 1996, 589.

45. Mote 1998, 186; Brownson 1995, 77; Hooson 1994, 140; Lishenyuk 1995, 28; Kempton 1996, 589.

46. Wescott 1997a, 14–21; 1997b, 24–28; Wood 1987; Rodgers 1990; Lishenyuk 1995, 40.

47. Jordan, Jordan-Bychkov, and Holz 1998; Sakha 1995b; Lishenyuk 1995, 8, 22, 34; Bauer, Kappeler, and Roth 1991, 225.

48. Khandakova 1992; Osadchiy 1993; Sivtsev 1992; Balzer 1995, 140.

49. Wescott 1997a.

50. Wein and Egorov 1992, 255–61; Vitebsky 1989; Vitebsky 1996, 105–6; Michael 1962, 40; Forsyth 1992, 176; Okladnikov 1970, 31; Williams 1997, A29, A34.

51. Jordan 1997.

## 2 · THE SNOW-MUFFLED VILLAGE

1. Semple 1911, 157.

2. Schmemann 1997, 12.

3. To sample the small body of literature on individual villages, see Wein and Egorov 1992; Schmemann 1997; Belov 1955; Humphrey 1983; Christobayev 1990; Jordan 1997; and Prosterman and Hanstad 1993.

4. *Demograficheskiye ezhegodnik* 1995; Sheehy 1986, 3.

5. Koutaniemi 1985; Berg 1950, 32. Suslov 1961, 195–96; *Atlas Sel'skogo* 1989, 10–11, 18–19, 48.

6. Sakha Republic 1995b; Lishenyuk 1995.

7. *Official Standard Names Gazetteer* 1970, 1: 210; Robinson 1949, 5.

8. "Russia: Eastern Part" 1996; *Official Standard Names Gazetteer* 1970, 1: 210; Poponin 1978, 472–73; Mote 1999.

9. Brownson 1995, 77.

10. "Demograficheskiye dannye" 1984–99.

11. Harris 1993, 595.

12. *Raspredeleniye naseleniya Rossii* 1995; Harris 1993, 572.

13. Rodgers 1990, 61; "Demograficheskiye dannye" 1984–99; *Demograficheskiye ezhegodnik* 1996, 34, 518.

14. Mote 1999; Lehmann 1998, 466–68, 473–74.

15. "Demograficheskiye dannye" 1984–99; *Atlas Sel'skogo* 1989, 92–93; Koutaniemi 1985, 421–25; Sergeev 1989, 92–96; *Agroklimaticheskiye* 1973, 7.

16. Seroshevsky 1993, 21.

17. Okladnikov 1970, 382.

18. Seroshevsky 1993, 24; Middendorff 1847–75, vol. 4, part 1, 392.

19. Seroshevsky 1993, 25.

20. Fedorov 1996, 99, 106–7; Vinogradova 1997, 75–76; Skryabin 1998, 200; Hughes et al. 1999.

21. Tikhonova 1997.

22. Seroshevsky 1993, 26.

23. *Agroklimaticheskiye* 1973, 9; Wein 1991, 196.

24. Müller 1882, 267–68; Wein 1991, 196.

25. Jochelson 1934, 81–82.

26. *Agroklimaticheskiye* 1973, 9; Berg 1950, 25, 360; Wein 1991, 196.

27. Savvinova 1997; Maak 1994, 346; Gmelin 1751–52, 2: 346.

28. Seroshevsky 1993, 27; *Agroklimaticheskiye* 1973, 11; Maak 1994, 417; Gmelin 1751–52, 2: 365; Wein 1991, 196.

29. Koutaniemi 1985, 428–30; Suslov 1961, 195–96; Federov 1996, 107; *Atlas Sel'skogo* 1989, 27.

30. Koutaniemi 1985, 425–26.

31. Koutaniemi 1985, 427–28.

32. Suslov 1961, 202; *Atlas Sel'skogo* 1989, 32–33; "Prirodno" 1980; "Eksplikatsiya" 1996; *Agroklimaticheskiye* 1973; Jochelson 1934, 82; Berg 1950, 35.

33. Wein 1997, 123.

34. Bagdarihihn-Syulbeh 1985, 42; 1997; Suslov 1961, 196; "Eksplikatsiya" 1996; "Prirodno" 1980; Middendorff 1847–75, vol. 3, part 2, 8, 56, 134; "Informatsiya" 1989; Maak 1994, 312.

35. Pakhomov 1997a, [2].

36. Seroshevsky 1993, 59.

37. Berg 1950, 42; Suslov 1961, 201.

38. Bagdarihihn-Syulbeh 1997.

39. Bagdarihihn-Syulbeh 1997; Balzer 1994, 406.

40. Suslov 1961, 201.

41. *Atlas Sel'skogo* 1989, 32–33; Elovskaya and Ivanov 1989, 97–101; "Prirodno" 1980, 12; Jochelson 1934, 82–83; Berg 1950, 34, 38–42; Suslov 1961, 201–2; Vrutzevich 1891, 38.

42. "Prirodno" 1980, 12.

# 3 · BEFORE A VILLAGE STOOD ON OYBON'S SHORE

1. Gmelin 1751–52, 2: 344–45; Okladnikov 1970, 235–45, 287290, 305–37; Jochelson 1934, 51; Strahlenberg 1738, 380; Antonov 1993; Middendorff 1847–75, vol. 3, parts 1 and 2; Balzer 1994, 404.

2. Gumilev 1990; Okladnikov 1954, 7–15; Middendorff 1847–75, vol. 4, part 2, 1409, 1545; Okladnikov 1970, 247, 265, 353, 377; Jochelson 1934, 221; Michael 1962; Gmelin 1751–52, 2: 344–45; Vinokurova 1994; Vitebsky 1990, 304–5.

3. Gogolev 1993, 108–10; Vorob'yev 1975, 79; Middendorff 1847–75, vol. 4, part 2, 1561; Gmelin 1751–52, 2: 344–45; Maak 1994, 375.

4. Strahlenberg 1738, 380; Bauer, Kappeler, and Roth 1991, 225; Slezkine 1994, 16, 65, 68; Jochelson 1934, 49–52, 64, 75, 220; Priklonskiy 1896; Vrutzevich 1891, 3; Bassin 1988; Collins 1982; Mostakhov 1982; Semyonov 1944; Bruk and Kabuzan 1989, 148; Hausladen 1989, 232–37; Coquin 1969; Treadgold 1957; Fondahl 1993, 497; Balzer 1994, 404.

5. Okladnikov 1970, 246–47; Tokarev and Gurvich 1964, 247, 269; Seroshevsky and Sumner 1901, 69; Jochelson 1934, 49; Strahlenberg 1738, 382.

6. Vrutzevich 1891, 28–29; Maak 1994, 254.

7. Maak 1994, 250–51. The quote came not from a formal interview, but rather from a conversation with a woman known to us simply as Nina.

8. Parker 1968, 135; Jochelson 1934, 64; Maak 1994, 196; Wein 1991, 195.

9. Jochelson 1934, 220; Michael 1962, 3–7; Remezov 1958, sheet 154; Dmytryshyn, Crownheart-Vaughan, and Vaughan 1985, 1: 172.

10. Maydell 1893–96, 2: 466; Gmelin 1751–52, 2: 384.

11. Ides 1706; Strahlenberg 1738; Middendorff 1847–75; Gmelin 1751–52, 2: 524–25, 3: folded map following 584; Maydell 1893–96, 2: 465; Dobell 1830; Müller 1882; Dmytryshyn, Crownheart-Vaughan, and Vaughan 1985, 1: 448 (quote).

12. Maak 1994, 52–53.

13. Okladnikov 1970, 421–23; Jochelson 1934, 48–49, 55.

14. Okladnikov 1970, 423, 433; Slezkine 1994, 28; Pakhomov 1997a, [1].

15. Seroshevsky 1993, 480; Maak 1994, 193, 513–55.

16. Maak 1994, 516–17.

17. Maak 1994, 311, 515–16, 555, 557, 560; Okladnikov 1970, 384–85; Seroshevsky 1993, 433; Tokarev and Gurvich 1964, 261–65.

18. Gmelin 1751–52, 2: 473; Jochelson 1934, 48; Middendorff 1847–75, vol. 4, part 2, 1559.

19. Maak 1994, 201–2; Müller 1882, 164–65; Strahlenberg 1738, 382; Jochelson 1934, 135–43; Okladnikov 1970, 383–84; Stenin 1897.

20. Semple 1911, 624; Jochelson 1934, 139; Okladnikov 1970, 384; Tokarev and Gurvich 1964, 263; Gmelin 1751–52, 2: 401–2; Maak 1994, 201–2; Middendorff 1847–75, vol. 4, part 2, 1560.

21. Bartenev and Fyodorov 1972; Opolovnikov and Opolovnikova 1983, 1989; Sivtsev 1992; Levin and Potapov 1961, 164.

22. Maak 1994, 187.

23. Strahlenberg 1738, 384–85; Maak 1994, 335–36; Mote 1999.

24. Maak 1994, 203, 335, 339–43.

25. Seroshevsky and Sumner 1901, 68–72; Tokarev and Gurvich 1964, 248; Okladnikov 1970, 237–38, 384; Jochelson 1934, 103; Gmelin 1751–52, 2: 470–71.

26. Basharin 1962, 111–14; Basharin 1956, 22, 24–25; Maak 1994, 325; Jochelson 1934, 188.

27. Dobell 1830, 1: 345 (quote); Middendorff 1847–75, vol. 4, part 2, 1562–63; Ivanov 1966, 41.

28. Maak 1994, 330–31; Graburn and Young 1973, 33; Seroshevsky and Sumner 1901, 65.

29. Maak 1994, 77, 331.

30. Strahlenberg 1738, 382; Gmelin 1751–52, 2: 550.

31. Dobell 1830, 1: 344; Jochelson 1934, 191.

32. Tokarev and Gurvich 1964, 248; Gmelin 1751–52, 2: 370.

33. Okladnikov 1970, 243.

34. Dobell 1830, 1: 343.

35. Tokarev and Gurvich 1964, 267–68; Maak 1994, 214.

36. Fedorova 1991, 9; Maak 1994, 213, 221–22, 259, 322, 325; Gmelin 1751–52, 2: 470–71; Dobell 1830, 1: 321, 325; Tokarev and Gurvich 1964, 267, 269; Jochelson 1934, 46; Seroshevsky and Sumner 1901, 70.

37. Gmelin 1751–52, 2: 478; Jochelson 1934, 46; Tokarev and Gurvich 1964, 267–69.

38. Strahlenberg 1738, 382.

39. Maak 1994, 205, 351.

40. Maak 1994, 331, 350, 351; Jochelson 1934, 142; Seroshevsky and Sumner 1901, 71; Dobell 1830, 1: 345; Bagdarihihn-Syulbeh 1997.

41. Maak 1994, 323, 351; Seroshevsky and Sumner 1901, 69, 74–75.

42. Vrutzevich 1891, 41.

43. Okladnikov 1970, 239; Jochelson 1934, 100, 188; Graburn and Young 1973, 33.

44. Dobell 1830, 1: 345.

45. Tokarev and Gurvich 1964, 248.

46. Seroshevsky and Sumner 1901, 66–67; Maak 1994, 351.

47. Seroshevsky 1993, 434; Jochelson 1934, 141–42; Okladnikov 1970, 384–85; Maak 1994, 205.

48. Strahlenberg 1738, 382–83.

49. Gmelin 1751–52, 2: 473; Tokarev and Gurvich 1964, 263–65.

50. Mikhailov and Yakovlev 1992, 152.

51. Schwarz 1961, 17; Ivanov 1966, 41.

52. Maak 1994, 263; Maydell 1893–96, 1: 464.

53. Maak 1994, 355–56; Gmelin 1751–52, 2: 471.

54. Maak 1994, 222; Gmelin 1751–52, 2: 471.

55. Maak 1994, 207–8.

56. Maak 1994, 355, 362.

57. Maak 1994, 356–59; Jochelson 1934, 35, 47; Tokarev and Gurvich 1964, 250–54.

58. Maak 1994, 363; Balzer 1994, 405.

59. Pavlov 1986, 570, 575; Middendorff 1847–75, vol. 4, part 2, 829; Maak 1994, 355; Okladnikov 1970, 385; Tokarev and Gurvich 1964, 247; Maydell 1893–96, 1: 463.

60. Maak 1994, 213, 363; Tokarev and Gurvich 1964, 267; Okladnikov 1970, 382.

61. Dobell 1830, 1: 344.
62. Maak 1994, 365.
63. Maak 1994, 364–65, 370; Fedorova 1991, 136, 154.
64. Tokarev and Gurvich 1964, 267; Middendorff 1847–75, vol. 4, part 1, 1565; Maak 1994, 216–17; Strahlenberg 1738, 382; Okladnikov 1970, 385; Seroshevsky and Sumner 1901, 67; Tokarev and Gurvich 1964, 254.
65. Gmelin 1751–52, 2: 469; Maak 1994, 218–19; Seroshevsky 1993, 307.
66. Maak 1994, 218; Gmelin 1751–52, 2: 464; Seroshevsky 1993, 308.
67. Seroshevsky 1993, 635–36.
68. Strahlenberg 1738, 382; Gmelin 1751–52, 2: 469; Müller 1882, 252–53.
69. Ides 1706, 36.
70. Strahlenberg 1738, 384; Dobell 1830, 2: 3, 21–22; Collins 1982, 30; Shunkov 1981, 611.
71. Jochelson 1934, 185; Tokarev and Gurvich 1964, 254; Basharin 1956.
72. Gmelin 1751–52, 2: 369, 519; Müller 1882, 251, 254.
73. Maak 1994, 216, 322, 345–47.
74. Maak 1994, 322, 345–46.
75. Maak 1994, 165, 350–51; Müller 1882, 255.
76. Jochelson 1934, 157–63; Okladnikov 1970, 385–87.
77. Tokarev and Gurvich 1964, 254–55.
78. Gmelin 1751–52, 2: 475; Maak 1994, 255.
79. Gmelin 1751–52, 2: 474; Müller 1882, 257–58; Jochelson 1934, 61; Seroshevsky 1993, 610; Mikhailov and Yakovlev 1992, 140.
80. Müller 1882, 258.
81. Maak 1994, 77; Levin and Potapov 1961, 54.
82. Tokarev and Gurvich 1964, 260.
83. Maak 1994, 77.
84. Dobell 1830, 1: 346.
85. Ides 1706, 36; Lehmann 1998, 466.
86. Strahlenberg 1738, 380.
87. Middendorff 1847–75, vol. 4, part 2, 1609.
88. Priklonskiy 1896, 42.
89. Maak 1994, 53, 513–55.
90. Jochelson 1934, 105.
91. Jochelson 1934, 103; Mote 1998, 71; Gogolev 1992.
92. Diószegi 1968; Diószegi and Hoppál 1978; Alekseev 1990; Ksenofontov 1992.
93. Czaplicka 1914, 277–79; Jochelson 1934, 103; Seroshevsky 1993, 629; Gogolev 1992; Balzer 1994, 406.
94. Jochelson 1906; Jochelson 1934, 97–217; Czaplicka 1914, 297–98; Maak 1994, 289; Balzer 1995, 145; Balzer 1994, 407.
95. Maak 1994, 314; Seroshevsky 1993, 616; Gmelin 1751–52, 2: 351–59; Balzer 1994, 406.
96. Gmelin 1751–52, 2: 356.
97. Jochelson 1934, 105.
98. Gogolev 1993.
99. Seroshevsky 1993, 628.
100. Gmelin 1751–52, 2: 477.
101. Graburn and Young 1973, 35.
102. Rasputin 1996, 56.
103. Seroshevsky and Sumner 1901, 69; Graburn and Young 1973, 36; Vrutzevich 1891, 19; Robinson 1949, 12–33.
104. Seroshevsky and Sumner 1901, 74.
105. Maak 1994, 321.
106. Seroshevsky 1993, 465.
107. Michael 1962, 34; Graburn and Young 1973, 35; Tokarev and Gurvich 1964, 274.

108. Czaplicka 1914, 141; Graburn and Young 1973, 35.
109. Seroshevsky 1993, 498.
110. Seroshevsky 1993, 498.

# 4 · SOVIET VILLAGE

1. *Istoriya* 1955–63, vol. 1; Danilov 1988, 48, 303–5; Tokarev and Gurvich 1964, 248, 287–88; Jochelson 1934, 225; Dmitriyeva 1989, 103.
2. "Yakutskaya ASSR" 1934, sheet 3; Armstrong 1967, 9.
3. Jefferson 1928.
4. On the collectivization movement, see Reston 1975; Belov 1955; Stuart 1972, 1984; Lewin 1968; Hedlund 1984, 54–57; Medvedev 1987, 61–122.
5. "Arkhivy po istorii" 1932–97; A. Yakovlev 1997; Tokarev and Gurvich 1964, 291.
6. "Demograficheskiye dannye" 1936–67; Petrov 1992, 92; "Arkhivy po istorii" 1932–97; Stuart 1972, 11, 13.
7. Slezkine 1994, 195 (quote); Wixman 1984, 220.
8. Conquest 1986.
9. Pakhomov 1997a, [2]. The reference is to *Burnt by the Sun,* a well-known Russian movie about Stalin's purge terror.
10. Tokarev and Gurvich 1964, 295.
11. Petrov 1992, 16.
12. Tokarev and Gurvich 1964, 295; A. Yakovlev 1997.
13. Tokarev and Gurvich 1964, 295.
14. Petrov 1992, 16; Wein 1991, 196.
15. "Arkhivy po istorii" 1932–97; Bauer, Kappeler, and Roth 1991, 245.
16. Bater 1996, 183–84; Hedlund 1984, 10; Stuart 1972, 231; Medvedev 1987, 163, 183.
17. Hedlund 1984, 95; Medvedev 1987, 176; "Demograficheskiye dannye" 1936–67.
18. "Arkhivy po istorii" 1932–97.
19. Pakhomov 1997a, [2–3]; Petrov 1992, 113, 116, 122, 299.
20. Pakhomov 1997a, [2–3].
21. Tokarev and Gurvich 1964, 291.
22. "Demograficheskiye dannye" 1936–67; "Arkhivy po istorii" 1932–97; Ioffe and Nefedova 1997, 60, 65.
23. "Arkhivy po istorii" 1932–97.
24. Demograficheskiye dannye" 1936–67; Ioffe and Nefedova 1997, 72.
25. "Demograficheskiye dannye" 1936–67.
26. "Demograficheskiye dannye" 1936–67; Armstrong 1967, 10.
27. Tokarev and Gurvich 1964, 291; Balzer 1994, 405.
28. Petrov 1992, 130.
29. "Arkhivy po istorii" (1932–97) places the creation of "Stalin" kolkhoz in 1948, but "Demograficheskiye dannye" (1936–67) continued to use the name "Budyonny" as late as 1950.
30. Bater 1996, 184; Medvedev 1987, 176.
31. "Arkhivy po istorii" 1932–97.
32. "Demograficheskiye dannye" 1936–67.
33. Kosmachev 1969.
34. "Mashinno-traktorny" 1960–66; Tokarev and Gurvich 1964, 291; Petrov 1992, 92; "Arkhivy po istorii" 1932–97; Hedlund 1984, 58, 95; Medvedev 1987, 176.
35. "Arkhivy po istorii" 1932–97.
36. Armstrong 1965, 10.
37. Armstrong 1967, 10–12; Gray 1990, 6; Medvedev 1987, 161–206; Stuart 1984, 273.
38. Bater 1996, 189; Armstrong 1967, 8.
39. Lydolph 1964; Dmitriyeva 1989; Ioffe and Nefedova 1997, 76–80; Armstrong 1965, 11; Popova 1978, 97; Wein 1991, 195.
40. "Arkhivy po istorii" 1932–97; Bater 1996, 189–91.
41. Popova 1978, 117.

42. Sallnow 1989, 674; "Demograficheskiye dannye" 1968–83, 1984–99.

43. "SSSR/RSFSR/Yakutskaya ASSR" 1980–82, "Arylaks" sheet; *Official Standard Names Gazetteer* 1970, 1: 210.

44. Pakhomov 1997a, [1].

45. Popova 1978, 13, 97, 101, 117; Yegorova 1994–95, 36–37; Stuart 1984, 243, 254; Malkhazova et al. 1997, 11; Marples 1999, 67–72.

46. "Demograficheskiye dannye" 1984–99; *Demograficheskiye ezhegodnik* 1996, 518.

47. Luk'yanov 1982, 523–24; Dmitriyeva 1989; Symons 1972; Korotov 1989.

48. "Demograficheskiye dannye" 1968–83; Hedlund 1984, 11, 86; Korotov 1989, 109; Wein 1991, 194.

49. Hedlund 1984, 1–3; Gray 1990, 6, 17; Christobayev 1990, 151–59; Stuart 1984, 286; Medvedev 1987, 334–46.

50. Wein 1991, 196.

51. "Mashinno-traktorny" 1988–99.

52. Wood 1987, 47.

53. Pakhomov 1997a, [1].

54. Balzer 1995, 145.

55. Tokarev and Gurvich 1964, 292; Shubnikova 1967; Kirikov 1983, 308–11; Armstrong 1965, 11.

# 5 · POST-SOVIET DJARKHAN

1. Demko, Ioffe, and Zayonchkovskaya 1999; Pakhomov 1995, 59; "Demograficheskiye dannye" 1984–99.

2. Ivanov 1997; *Demograficheskiy ezhegodnik* 1995, 430; 1996, 518; "Demograficheskiye dannye" 1984–99; *Chislennost'* 1991, 1998.

3. Demograficheskiye dannye" 1984–99; Popova 1996.

4. *Demograficheskiy ezhegodnik* 1996, 34, 101; 1997, 99; "Demograficheskiye dannye" 1984–99.

5. Craumer 1994, 333–34, 342, 345; Bater 1996, 177, 203–8; Pakhomov 1995, 163–65.

6. Ivanov 1997; Yakovlev 1997; "Eksplikatsiya" 1996.

7. "Zapisi" 1993–97.

8. Pakhomov 1997b; Ivanov 1997.

9. Myreyev 1996.

10. Ivanov 1997.

11. Pakhomov 1997b; Ivanov 1997.

12. Ivanov 1997.

13. Sivtsev 1997; Ivanov 1997; "Demograficheskiye dannye" 1984–99; Wines 1998, A10.

14. Ioffe and Nefedova 1997, 165; Sivtsev 1997; "Zapisi" 1993–97.

15. "Premier of Russia" 1997, A8.

16. "Mashinno" 1988–99; Ivanov 1997; Craumer 1994, 333, 345; "Demograficheskiye dannye" 1984–99.

17. Pakhomov 1997b; Ivanov 1997; "Demograficheskiye dannye" 1984–99.

18. Kondratiev 1996; Craumer 1994, 333.

19. Ivanov 1997.

20. "Demograficheskiye dannye" 1984–99; Ivanov 1997; Savvinova 1997; Pakhomov 1998a.

21. Ivanov 1997; "Eksplikatsiya" 1996.

22. "Demograficheskiye dannye" 1984–99; Ivanov 1997.

23. Tikhomirov 1997, 155–69, 193, 197.

24. Malkhazova et al. 1997, 11; Petrov 1997; Ivanov 1997; *Demograficheskiy ezhegodnik* 1995, 98, 234; 1996, 112, 266; 1997, 110, 265; "Demograficheskiye dannye" 1984–99.

25. Wescott 1997b, 29; Brownson 1995, 77.

26. "Mashinno" 1988–99.

27. Ivanov 1997.

28. Pakhomov 1997b; "Demograficheskiye dannye" 1984–99.

29. Ivanov 1997; Pakhomov 1998b.

30. Balzer and Vinokurova 1996, 104; Balzer 1997, 38–39; Lehmann 1998, 466–68.

31. Tikhonova 1996.

## 6 · DO NOT VANISH, MY VILLAGE

1. Brownson 1995, 77.
2. Pakhomov 1997b.
3. Ioffe and Nefedova 1997, 125–28.
4. Wescott 1997b, 27; Brownson 1995, 77.
5. Ioffe and Nefedova 1997, 280.
6. Pakhomov 1997a, [3]; Pakhomov 1997b.
7. Artamonov 1997.
8. Williams 1997, A34.
9. Pakhomov 1997a, 1997b, 1998a.
10. Ivanov 1997.
11. Pakhomov 1997b.
12. Ivanov 1997; Pakhomov 1997b.
13. Denisova 1995, 2–3.
14. "Demograficheskiye dannye" 1968–83; Denisova 1995, 97.
15. Vil'chek, Serebryannyy, and Tishkov 1996, 249–66.
16. O'Brien et al. 1993, 11–20.
17. Pakhomov 1997a, [3–5], 1997b.
18. Pika and Prokhorov 1994.
19. Fondahl 1997, 203; Slezkine 1994; Vitebsky 1989; Williams 1997.
20. Pakhomov 1995, 18; Fondahl 1993, 480, 486.
21. Pakhomov 1995, 201.
22. Pakhomov 1997b.
23. Tuan 1974.
24. Tuan 1976, 12; Tuan 1980.
25. Walter 1988, 115.
26. Denisova 1995, 155.
27. Hay 1998, 246.
28. Williams 1997.
29. Ivanov 1997; Pakhomov 1997a, [4].
30. Pakhomov 1998b.
31. Williams 1997, A34.
32. Pakhomov 1995, 245.
33. Pakhomov 1998a, Savvinova 1997.
34. Pakhomov 1997b.
35. Pakhomov 1995, 59.
36. Pakhomov 1997b.
37. Denisova 1995, 92.
38. Pakhomov 1998b; Ivanov 1999; Popova 1999, 2000.
39. Pakhomov 1998a; *Demograficheskiye ezhegodnik* 1996, 34.
40. Pakhomov 1995, 193.

# REFERENCES

*Agroklimaticheskiye resursy Yakutskoy ASSR* (Agroclimatological Resources of the Yakut ASSR; in Russian). 1973. Leningrad: Gidrometeoizdat.

Alekseev, N. A. 1990. "Shamanism among the Turkic Peoples of Siberia." In Marjorie M. Balzer (ed.), *Shamanism: Soviet Studies of Traditional Religion in Siberia and Central Asia.* Armonk, NY: M. E. Sharpe, 49–109.

Antonov, N. K. 1993. *Naslediye predkov* (The Ancestral Legacy; in Russian). Yakutsk: "Bichik."

Arievich, G. 1992. "Komu kurit' almaznuyu trubku?" (Who Will Smoke the Diamond Pipe?; in Russian). *Novoye Vremya* 6 (February): 37–38.

Argounova, Tatiana, and Joachim O. Habeck. 1997–98. "Republic of Sakha (Yakutia)." Scott Polar Research Institute, University of Cambridge, Web site: <http://www.spri.com.ac.uk/rfn/sakha.htm>.

"Arkhivy po istorii Djarkhana" (Archives on the History of Djarkhan; in Russian). 1932–97. Records in the village council hall, Djarkhan, Sakha.

Armstrong, Terence E. 1965. "Visit to the USSR, September–October 1965 with Notes on the Yakutskaya ASSR." Unpublished, confidential report prepared for the United States government by a faculty member of the Scott Polar Research Institute, Cambridge, MA. 14 pp. Copy in possession of the authors.

Armstrong, Terence E. 1967. "Visit to the USSR, July 1967, with Notes on Yakutskaya ASSR." Unpublished, confidential report prepared for the United States government by a faculty member of the Scott Polar Research Institute, Cambridge, MA. 16 pp. Copy in possession of the authors.

Artamonov, Vitaly P. 1997. Interview by the authors with the Minister of Foreign Relations of the Sakha Republic, at Yakutsk, June 24.

*Atlas Sel'skogo Khozyaystva Yakutskoy ASSR* (Agricultural Atlas of the Yakut ASSR; in Russian). 1989. Moscow: Glavnoye upravleniye Geodeziye i Kartografiye pri Sovete Ministrov SSSR.

Azulay, Eric, and Allegra Harris Azulay. 1995. *The Russian Far East.* New York: Hippocrene Books.

Bagdarihihn-Syulbeh (pseud. for Mikhail S. Ivanov). 1985. *Toponimika Yakutii* (Yakutian Placenames; in Russian). Yakutsk: Yakutskoye Knizhoye Izdatel'stvo.

———. 1997. Interview by the authors with Sakha's leading toponymic expert, at Yakutsk, July 21.

Balzer, Marjorie Mandelstam. 1994. "Yakut." In *Encyclopedia of World Cultures.* Vol. 6. Edited by Paul Friedrich and Norma Diamond. Boston: G. K. Hall, 404–7.

———. 1995. "A State within a State: The Sakha Republic (Yakutia)." In Stephen Kotkin and David Wolff (eds.), *Rediscovering Russia in Asia: Siberia and the Russian Far East.* Armonk, NY: M. E. Sharpe, 139–59.

———. 1997. "Soviet Superpower." *Natural History* 106(2): 38–39.

———. 1999. *The Tenacity of Ethnicity: A Siberian Saga in Global Perspective.* Princeton, NJ: Princeton University Press.

Balzer, Majorie Mandelstam, and Uliana Alekseevna Vinokurova. 1996. "Nationalism, Interethnic Relations, and Federalism: The Case of the Sakha Republic." *Europe-Asia Studies* 48: 101–20.

Bartenev, Igor A., and B. Fyodorov. 1972. *North Russian Architecture.* Moscow: Progress Publishers.

Basharin, G. P. 1956. *Istoriya agrarnykh otnosheniy v Yakutii, 60-e gody XVIII-ser.XIX v* (History of Agrarian Relations in Yakutia, 1760s to the Middle Nineteenth Century; in Russian). Moscow: Izdatel'stvo Akademii Nauk SSSR.

———. 1962. *Istoriya zhivotnovodstva v Yakutii vtoroy poloviny XIX-nachala XX v* (History of Livestock Raising in Yakutia from the Last Half of the Nineteenth Century to the Early Twentieth Century; in Russian). Yakutsk: Yakutskoye Knizhnoye Izdatel'stvo.

Bassin, Mark. 1988. "Expansion and Colonialism on the Eastern Frontier: Views of Siberia and the Far East in Pre-Petrine Russia." *Journal of Historical Geography* 14: 3–21.

———. "Russia between Europe and Asia: The Ideological Construction of Geographical Space." *Slavic Review* 50: 1–17.

Bater, James H. 1996. *Russia and the Post-Soviet Scene: A Geographical Perspective.* London: Arnold.

Bater, James H., and R. A. French (eds.) 1983. *Studies in Russian Historical Geography.* 2 vols. London: Academic Press.

Bauer, Henning, Andreas Kappeler, and Brigitte Roth (eds.). 1991. *Die Nationalitäten des Russischen Reiches in der Volkszählung von 1897.* Stuttgart, Germany: Franz Steiner.

Belov, Fedor. 1955. *The History of a Soviet Collective Farm.* New York: Praeger.

Berg, Lev S. 1950. *Natural Regions of the USSR.* New York: Macmillan.

Bosikov, N. P. 1991. *Evolyutsiya Alasov Tsentralnoy Iakutii* (Evolution of the Alases of Central Yakutia; in Russian). Yakutsk: Permafrost Institute.

Bradshaw, Michael J. 1992. *Siberia at a Time of Change.* London: The Economist Intelligence Unit.

Bradshaw, Michael J., and Nicholas J. Lynn. 1998. "Resource-Based Development in the Russian Far East: Problems and Prospects." *Geoforum* 29: 375–92.

Brownson, J. M. Jamil. 1995. *In Cold Margins: Sustainable Development in Northern Bioregions.* Missoula, MT: Northern Rim Press.

Bruk, S. I., and V. M. Kabuzan. 1989. "The Dynamics and Ethnic Composition of the Population of Russia in the Era of Imperialism." *Soviet Geography* 30: 130–54.

Chinn, Jeff, and Robert Kaiser. 1996. *Russians as the New Minority: Ethnicity and Nationalism in the Soviet Successor States.* Boulder, CO: Westview Press.

*Chislennost' naseleniya RSFSR po gorodam rabochim poselkam i rayonam na 1. Yanvarya 1991 g.* (Population of the RSFSR at the Level of Cities, Industrial Towns, and Counties, January 1, 1991; in Russian). 1991. Moscow: Goskomstat RSFSR.

*Chislennost' naseleniya Rossiyskoy Federatsii po gorodam, poselkam gorodskogo tipa i rayonam na 1. Yanvarya 1998 g.* (Population of the Russian Federation at the Level of Cities, Towns, and Counties, January 1, 1998; in Russian). 1998. Moscow: Goskomstat Rossii.

Christobayev, A. I. 1990. "A State Farm in the Depths of the Nonchernozem Zone." *Soviet Geography* 31: 151–59.

Clem, Ralph S., and Peter R. Craumer. 1995. "The Politics of Russia's Regions." *Post-Soviet Geography* 36: 67–86.

Cole, John P. 1991. "Republics of the Former USSR in the Context of a United Europe and New World Order." *Soviet Geography* 32: 587–603.

Collins, David N. 1982. "Russia's Conquest of Siberia." *European Studies Review* 12: 17–44.

Conquest, Robert. 1986. *The Harvest of Sorrow: Soviet Collectivization and the Terror-Famine.* New York: Oxford University Press.

Coquin, François-X. 1969. *La Siberie: Peuplement et immigration paysanne au XIXe siècle.* Paris: Institut d'Etudes Slaves.

Craumer, Peter R. 1994. "Regional Patterns of Agricultural Reform in Russia." *Post-Soviet Geography* 35: 329–51.

Czaplicka, M. A. 1914. *Aboriginal Siberia.* Oxford, England: Clarendon Press.

Danilov, Victor P. 1988. *Rural Russia under the New Regime.* Translated by Orlando Figes. London: Hutchinson.

Demko, George J., Grigory Ioffe, and Zhanna Zayonchkovskaya (eds.). 1999. *Population under Duress: The Geodemography of Post-Soviet Russia.* Boulder, CO: Westview Press.

"Demograficheskiye dannye Vtorogo Djarkhanskogo Naslega" (Demographic Data of the Second Djarkhan District; in Russian). 1936–67. Manuscript annual censuses of population and agriculture. In the Suntar Ulus regional archives, Suntar, Sakha.

"Demograficheskiye dannye Djarkhanskogo Naslega" (Demographic Data of the Djarkhan District; in Russian). 1968–83. Manuscript annual censuses of population and agriculture. In the Suntar Ulus regional archive, Suntar, Sakha.

"Demograficheskiye dannye sela Djarkhan" (Demographic Data of Djarkhan; in Russian). 1984–99. Manuscript annual censuses, in the village council hall, Djarkhan, Sakha.

*Demograficheskiye ezhegodnik Rossiiskoy Federatsii* (Demographic Yearbook of the Russian Federation; in Russian and English). 1993, 1994. Moscow: Goskomstat Rossii.

*Demograficheskiye ezhegodnik Rossii* (Demographic Yearbook of Russia; in Russian and English). 1995, 1996, 1997, 1998, 1999. Moscow: Goskomstat Rossii.

Denisova, L. N. 1995. *Rural Russia: Economic, Social, and Moral Crisis.* Commack, NY: Nova Science Publishers.

Denisova, L. N. 1996. *Ischezayushchaya Derevnya Rossii:Nechernozem'ye v 1960–1980-e Godiy* (Disappearing Villages of Russia: The Non-Chernozem Region, 1960–1980s; in Russian). Moscow: Institut Rossiiysoy Istorii PAH.

Diószegi, Vilmos (ed.). 1968. *Popular Beliefs and Folklore Tradition in Siberia*. Bloomington, IN: Indiana University Press.

Diószegi, Vilmos, and M. Hoppál (eds.). 1978. *Shamanism in Siberia*. Budapest: Akademiai Kiado.

Dmitrieva, Z. M. 1989. "Naseleniye" (Population). In *Atlas Sel'skogo Khozyaystva Yakutskoy ASSR* (Agricultural Atlas of the Yakut ASSR; in Russian). 1989. Moscow: Glavnoye upravleniye Geodeziye i Kartografiye pri Sovete Ministrov SSSR, 102–4.

Dmytryshyn, Basil, E., A. P. Crownheart-Vaughan, and Thomas Vaughan (eds. and trans.). 1985. *Russia's Conquest of Siberia, 1558–1700: A Documentary Record*. Vol. 1. Portland, OR: Oregon Historical Society Press.

Dobell, Peter. 1830. *Travels in Kamchatka and Siberia*. 2 vols. London: Henry Colburn and Richard Bentley.

Dostál, Petr, and H. Knippenberg. 1979. "The Russification of Ethnic Minorities in the USSR." *Soviet Geography* 20: 197–219.

Drobizheva, L. 1995. *Etnopoliticheskaya situatsiya i mezhnatsional'nyye otnosheniya v respublikakh Rossiyskoy Federastii* (The Ethnic and Political Situation, and Interethnic Relations in the Republics of the Russian Federation; in Russian). Moscow: Institut Etnologii i Antropologii.

Dwyer, Denis, and David Drakakis-Smith (eds.). 1996. *Ethnicity and Development: Geographical Perspectives*. Chichester, England: Wiley.

"Eksplikatsiya zemel' otdeleniy, sovkhozov" (Explications of the Division of Sovkhoz Lands; in Russian). 1996. Report in the village council hall, Djarkhan, Sakha.

Elovskaya, L. G., and I. A. Ivanov. 1989. "Pochvy" (Soils). In *Atlas Sel'skogo Khozyaystva Yakutskoy ASSR* (Agricultural Atlas of the Yakut ASSR; in Russian). 1989. Moscow: Glavnoye upravleniye Geodeziye i Kartografiye pri Sovete Ministrov SSSR, 97–101.

Espenshade, Edward B. Jr., John C. Hudson, and Joel L. Morrison (eds.). 1995. *Goode's World Atlas*. 19th ed. Chicago: Rand McNally.

Fedorov, A. N. 1996. "Effects of Recent Climate Change on Permafrost Landscapes in Central Sakha." *Polar Geography* 20: 99–108.

Fedorova, V. N. 1991. *Blyuda Narodov Yakutii* (Cuisine of the Peoples of Yakutia; in Russian). Yakutsk: Yakutskoye Knizhnoye Izdatel'stvo.

*First Book of Demographics for the Republics of the Former Soviet Union, 1951–1990*. 1992. Shady Side, MD: New World Demographics.

Fondahl, Gail A. 1993. "Siberia: Native Peoples and Newcomers in Collision." In Ian Bremmer and Ray Taras (eds.), *Nations and Politics in the Soviet Successor States*. Cambridge, England: Cambridge University Press, 477–510.

———. 1997. "Siberia: Assimilation and Its Discontents." In Ian Bremmer and Ray Taras (eds.), *New States, New Politics: Building the Post-Soviet Nations*. Cambridge, England: Cambridge University Press, 190–232.

Forsyth, James. 1992. *A History of the Peoples of Siberia*. Cambridge, England: Cambridge University Press.

Gmelin, J. G. 1751–52. *D. Johann Georg Gmelins Reise durch Sibirien von dem Jahr 1733 bis 1743*. 3 vols. Göttingen, Germany: A. Vandenhoeck.

Gogolev, Anatoliy I. 1992. "Intuitivnoye i logicheskoye v naturphilosofskikh predstavleniyakh yakutov" (Intuitive and Logical Elements in the Nature Philosophy of the Yakuts; in Russian). In: A. G. Novikov (ed.), *Logos, kultura i tsivilizatsiya* (Logos, Culture, and Civilization; in Russian). Yakutsk: Yakut State University Press.

Gogolev, Anatoliy I. 1993. *Yakuty. Problemy etnogenesa i formirovaniya kultury* (The Yakuts. Problems of Ethnogenesis and Culture Formation; in Russian). Yakutsk: Yakut State University Press.

Graburn, Nelson H. H., and B. Stephen Young. 1973. "A Chiefdom of the Northern Yakuts." In Graburn, Nelson H. H., and B. Stephen Young, *Circumpolar Peoples*. Pacific Palisades, CA: Goodyear, 33–37.

Gray, Kenneth R. (ed.). 1990. *Soviet Agriculture: Comparative Perspectives*. Ames: Iowa State University Press.

Gumilev, Leo. 1990. *Ethnogenesis and the Biosphere*. Moscow: Progress Publishers.

Harris, Chauncy D. 1993. "A Geographical Analysis of Non-Russian Minorities in Russia and Its Ethnic Homelands." *Post-Soviet Geography* 34: 543–97.

Hauner, Milan. 1990. *What Is Asia to Us?* Boston: Unwin Hyman.

Hausladen, Gary. 1989. "Russian Siberia: An Integrative Approach." *Soviet Geography* 30: 231–46.

Hay, Robert. 1998. "A Rooted Sense of Place in Cross-Cultural Perspective." *Canadian Geographer* 42: 245–66.

Hedlund, Stefan. 1984. *Crisis in Soviet Agriculture*. London: Croom Helm.

Heleniak, Timothy. 1999. "Out-Migration and Depopulation of the Russian North during the 1990s." *Post-Soviet Geography and Economics* 40: 155–205.

Hiller, Kristin, and Sergei Kaptilkin. 1997. "Big River of Siberia." *Russian Life* 40 (9): 16–23.

Hooson, David (ed.). 1994. *Geography and National Identity.* Oxford, England: Blackwell.

Hughes, M. K., E. A. Vaganov, S. Shiyatov, R. Touchan, and G. Funkhouser. 1999. "Twentieth-Century Summer Warmth in Northern Yakutia in a 600-Year Context." *Holocene* 9: 629–34.

Humphrey, Caroline. 1983. *The Karl Marx Collective: Economy, Society, and Religion in a Siberian Collective Farm.* Cambridge, England: Cambridge University Press.

Ides, E. Ysbrants. 1706. *Three Years' Travels from Moscow Over-land to China.* London: W. Freeman.

"Informatsiya o dorogakh, postroykakh, vodoyomakh i inzhenernom obespecheniyi sela Djarkhan" (Information on Roads, Buildings, Lakes, and Heating Facilities in Djarkhan; in Russian). 1989. Report in the village council hall, Djarkhan, Sakha.

Ioffe, Grigory, and Tatyana Nefedova. 1997. *Continuity and Change in Rural Russia: A Geographic Perspective.* Boulder, CO: Westview Press.

*Istoriya Yakutskoy ASSR* (History of the Yakut ASSR; in Russian). 1955–63. 3 vols. Moscow: Akademia Nauk SSSR, Institut istorii.

Ivanov, Arkady N. 1997. Interview by the authors with the head of the Djarkhan Village Council, at Djarkhan, Sakha, July 8.

———1999. Personal letter in Russian to the authors, from Djarkhan, Sakha, October 7.

Ivanov, B. H. 1966. "K voprosy ob obraze zhizni Yakutov XVII v". (On the Way of Life of Yakuts in the Seventeenth Century; in Russian). *Yakutskiy Arkhiv* 3: 37–45.

Ivanov, Mikhail S. *See* Bagdarihihn-Syulbeh.

Jefferson, Mark. 1928. "The Civilizing Rails." *Economic Geography* 4: 217–31.

Jochelson, Waldemar. 1906. "Kumiss Festivals of the Yakuts and the Decoration of Kumiss Vessels." In *Boas Anniversary Volume: Anthropological Papers Written in Honor of Franz Boas.* New York: G. E. Stechert, 257–71.

———. 1934. "The Yakuts." *Anthropological Papers of the American Museum of Natural History* 33: 35–225.

Jordan, Bella Bychkova. 1997. "Djarkhan, a Siberian Village: Rural Life and Land in the Sakha Republic." Master of Arts thesis. University of Texas at Austin.

Jordan, Bella Bychkova, Terry G. Jordan-Bychkov, and Robert K. Holz. 1998. "Post-Soviet Change in a Yakutian Farm Village." *Erdkunde* 52: 219–31.

Kaiser, Robert J. 1994. *The Geography of Nationalism in Russia and the U.S.S.R.* Princeton, NJ: Princeton University Press.

———. 1995. "Prospects for the Disintegration of the Russian Federation." *Post-Soviet Geography* 36: 426–35.

Kempton, Daniel R. 1996. "The Republic of Sakha (Yakutia): The Evolution of Centre-Periphery Relations in the Russian Federation." *Europe-Asia Studies* 48: 587–613.

Khandakova, Z. A. 1992. *Nauka v Yakutskom Gosudarstvennom Universitete imeni M.K. Ammosova* (Science at the M.K. Ammosov Yakut State University; in Russian). Yakutsk: Yakut State University Press.

Kirikov, S. V. 1983. "Past and Present Distribution of Game Animals in the USSR." *Soviet Geography: Review and Translation* 24(4): 305–11.

Klyuchevsky, Aleksei B. 1989. "Recent Developments in Yakutia." In Alexander Bon and Robert van Voren (eds.), *Nationalism in the USSR: Problems of Nationalities.* Amsterdam, Netherlands: Second World Center, 107–10.

Kolossov, Vladimir. 1993. "Nationalism versus World Society: A View from Russia." In Peter J. Taylor (ed.), *Political Geography of the Twentieth Century: A Global Analysis.* London: Belhaven Press, 239–43.

Kondratiev, Vladimir. 1996. Interview by the authors with independent peasant farmer, in Djarkhan, Sakha, July 25.

Korotov, G. P. et al., 1989. "Zhivotnovodstvo" (Livestock Husbandry). In *Atlas Sel'skogo Khozyaystva Yakutskoy ASSR* (Agricultural Atlas of the Yakut ASSR; in Russian). 1989. Moscow: Glavnoye upravleniye Geodeziye i Kartografiye pri Sovete Ministrov SSSR, 109–10.

Kosmachev, K. P. 1969. "A Study of the Shapes of Economic Phenomena for the Purpose of Elaborating More Rational Techniques for the Opening up of Tayga Territories." *Soviet Geography: Review and Translation* 10: 603–12.

Koutaniemi, Leo. 1985. "The Central Yakutian Lowlands: Land of Climate Extremes, Permafrost and Alas Depressions." *Soviet Geography* 26: 421–36.

Krasikov, I. 1991. "Yakutiya—bezyadernaya zona" (Yakutia—Non-Nuclear Zone; in Russian). *Trud* (newspaper) (November 30).

Kraus, Michael, and Ronald D. Liebowitz (eds.). 1996. *Russia and Eastern Europe After Communism.* Boulder, CO: Westview Press.

Ksenofontov, G. V. 1992. *Shamanizm. Izbranniye trudy* (Shamanism. Selected Articles; in Russian). Yakutsk: "Sever-Yug."

———. 1993. *Urankhai Sakhalar* (Urankhai Yakuts; in Russian). 2 vols. Yakutsk: "Natsional'noye izdatel'stvo."

Lehmann, Susan G. 1998. "Inter-Ethnic Conflict in the Republics of Russia in Light of Religious Revival." *Post-Soviet Geography and Economics* 39: 461–93.

Levin, Maksim G., and L. P. Potapov. 1961. *Istoriko-etnograficheskiy Atlas Sibiri* (Historical and Ethnic Atlas of Siberia; in Russian). Moscow and Leningrad: Izdatel'stvo Akademii Nauk SSSR.

———. 1964. *The Peoples of Siberia.* Chicago: University of Chicago Press.

Lewin, Moshe. 1968. *Russian Peasants and Soviet Power: A Study of Collectivization.* Translated by Irene Nove and John Biggart. Evanston, IL: Northwestern University Press.

Lewis, Robert A., Richard H. Rowland, and Ralph S. Clem. 1976. *Nationality and Population Change in Russia and the USSR: An Evaluation of Census Data, 1897–1970.* New York: Praeger.

Linge, G. J. R. 1992. "Developments in Russia's Far East and Their Implications for the Pacific Basin." *Australian Geographical Studies* 30: 125–41.

Lishenyuk, S. N. (ed.). 1995. *Republic of Sakha: Yakutian Business Guide.* Yakutsk: Ministry of Foreign Relations.

Lobanov-Rostovsky, A. 1965. "Russian Expansion in the Far East in the Light of the Turner Hypothesis." In Walker D. Wyman and Clifton B. Kroeber (eds.), *The Frontier in Perspective.* Madison, WI: University of Wisconsin Press, 79–94.

Luk'yanov, Y. M. 1982. "Economic Linkages of the West Yakutian Diamond Area." *Soviet Geography: Review and Translation* 23(7): 521–24.

Lydolph, Paul E. 1964. "The Russian Sukhovey." *Annals of the Association of American Geographers* 54: 291–309.

———. 1977. *Climates of the Soviet Union.* Amsterdam: Elsevier.

———. 1990. *Geography of the U.S.S.R.* 5th ed. Elkhart Lake, WI: Misty Valley Publishing.

Lynn, Nicholas J., and Paul Fryer. 1998. "National-Territorial Change in the Republics of the Russian North." *Political Geography* 17: 567–88.

Maak, Richard Karlovich. 1994. *Vilyuyskiy Okrug* (Vilyuisk District; in Russian). Moscow: Yana. Originally published in 3 volumes in 1883–1887 under the longer title, *Vilyuyskiy Okrug Yakutskoy Oblasti* (The Vilyuisk District of the Yakutsk Territory).

Malkhazova, Svetlana M. et al. 1997. "Public Health and Environmental Pollution in Russia." *Bulletin, International Geographical Union* 47(1): 5–16.

Marples, David R. 1999. "Environmental and Health Problems in the Sakha Republic." *Post-Soviet Geography and Economics* 40: 62–77.

"Mashinno-traktorny park sela Djarkhan" (Registry of Motor Vehicles in Djarkhan; in Russian). 1988–99. Records in the village council hall, Djarkhan, Sakha.

"Mashinno-traktorny park, Kolkhoza imeni 'Lenina'." (Registry of Motor Vehicles in the "Lenin" Collective Farm; in Russian). 1960–66. Records in the Suntar *ulus* regional archives, Suntar, Sakha.

Maydell, Gerhard. 1893–96. *Reisen und Forschungen im jakutskischen Gebiet Ostsibiriens in den Jahren 1861–1871.* 2 vols. St. Petersburg: Commissionäre der Kaiserlichen Akademie der Wissenschaften.

Medvedev, Zhores A. 1987. *Soviet Agriculture.* New York: W. W. Norton.

Michael, Henry N. (ed.). 1962. *Studies in Siberian Ethnogenesis.* Toronto: University of Toronto Press.

Middendorff, Aleksandr Theodor von. 1847–75. *Reise in den äussersten Norden und Osten Sibiriens während der Jahre 1843 und 1844.* 4 volumes plus atlas. St. Petersburg: Buchdruckerei der Kaiserlichen Akademie der Wissenschaften.

Mikhailov, Aleksei, and Victor Yakovlev. 1992. *Yakutia.* Yakutsk: National Committee for Traditional and Official Events, Republic of Sakha. In Yakut and English.

Milner-Gulland, Robin, and Nikolai Dejevsky. 1989. *Cultural Atlas of Russia and the Soviet Union*. New York: Facts on File.

Mostakhov, S. E. 1982. *Russkiye puteshestvenniki-issledovateli Yakutii XVII-nach. XXV.* (Russian Travelers-Explorers of Yakutia, from the Seventeenth to Early Twentieth Centuries; in Russian). Yakutsk: Yakutsk Publishing House.

Mote, Victor L. 1998. *Siberia: Worlds Apart*. Boulder, CO: Westview Press.

Mote, Victor L. 1999. Letter (e-mail) to the authors, November 19, from Houston, Texas.

Müller, Ferdinand. 1882. *Unter Tungusen und Jakuten: Erlebnisse und Ergebnisse der Olenék-Expedition*. Leipzig: F. A. Brockhaus.

Murzayev, E. M. 1964. "Where Should One Draw the Geographical Boundary Between Europe and Asia?" *Soviet Geography: Review and Translation* 5: 15–25.

Myreyev, Alfanasy. 1996. Interview by the authors with the elected leader of the farm cooperative, Djarkhan, Sakha, July 23.

Nansen, Fridtjof. 1914. *Sibirien, ein Zukunftsland*. Leipzig: F. A. Brockhaus.

O'Brien, David J., Valery V. Patsiorkovsky, Inna Korkhova, and Larry Dershem. 1993. "The Future of the Village in a Restructured Food and Agricultural Sector in the Former Soviet Union." *Agriculture and Human Values* 10: 11–20.

*Official Standard Names Gazetteer, U.S.S.R.* 1970. 2nd ed. No. 42. 7 vols. Washington, DC: U.S. Army Topographic Command, Geographic Names Division,

Okladnikov, A. P. 1954. "Novyye arkheologicheskiye otkrytiya v vostochnoy Sibiri i drevnyaya istoriya Yakutii" (New Archaeological Findings in Eastern Siberia and the Ancient History of Yakutia; in Russian). *Papers*, 5th and 6th sessions, History and Philology, Yakutian Filial AN SSSR, 7–15.

Okladnikov, A. P. 1970. *Yakutia before Its Incorporation into the Russian State*. Montreal: McGill-Queen's University Press.

O'Loughlin, John, and Herman van der Wusten (eds.). 1993. *The New Political Geography of Eastern Europe*. London: Belhaven Press.

Opolovnikov, Alexsandr, and Yelena Opolovnikova. 1983. *Derevyannoye zodchestvo Yakutii* (Wooden Architecture of Yakutia; in Russian). Yakutsk: Yakutsk Publishing House.

Opolonikov, Alexsandr, and Yelena Opolonikova. 1989. *The Wooden Architecture of Russia: Houses, Fortifications, Churches*. New York: Harry N. Abrams.

Osadchiy, Victor (ed.). 1993. *Yakutsk, 1632–1992*. Moskva: "Taiga-Tsentr."

Pakhomov, A. K. 1993. *Sakha Sirin istoriatyn kepsennyar* (Glimpses of Yakutian History; in Yakutian). Yakutsk: "Bichik."

Pakhomov, Innokentiy. 1995. *Oy-Sanaa Tyuhyumehtere: Tya sirigyer reforma 1989–1994 SS.* (Thoughts about the Future of Villages in Sakha: Land Reform in Rural Sakha, 1989–1994; in Yakutian). Yakutsk: "Bichik."

———. 1997a. "Djaarkhan nehilegya: urukkuta uonna bilingite" (Djarkhan Village: Past and Future; in Yakutian). Pamphlet of 5 unnumbered pages. Yakutsk: Privately printed by author.

———. 1997b. Interview by the authors with the head of the Sakha Republic Committee for Land Reform, at Yakutsk, June 25.

———. 1998a. Interview by the authors with the head of the Sakha Republic Committee for Land Reform, at Yakutsk, June 29.

———. 1998b. Interview by the authors with the head of the Sakha Republic Committee for Land Reform, at Moscow, December 10.

Parker, W. H. 1960. "Europe: How Far?" *Geographical Journal* 126: 278–97.

———. 1968. *An Historical Geography of Russia*. London: University of London Press.

Pavlov, P. N. 1986. "Fur Trade in the Economy of Siberia in the 17th Century." *Soviet Geography* 27: 567–90.

Petrov, D. D. 1992. *Yakutiya v gody Velikoy Otechestvennoy voyny (Yakutia in the Years of the Great Patriotic War; in Russian)*. Pt. 2. Yakutsk: Knizhnoye Izdatel'stvo.

Petrov, L. A. 1997. Interview by the authors with the chief surgeon, Suntar Regional Hospital, Suntar, Sakha, July 27.

Pika, Aleksandr and Boris Prokhorov. 1994. *Neotraditsionalizm na Rossiyskom Severe: etnicheskoye vozrozhdeniye malochislennykh narodov severa i gosudarstvennaya regional'naya politika*

(Neotraditionalism in the Russian North: Ethnic Revival of the Small Peoples of the North and Governmental Regional Policy; in Russian). Moscow: Center for Demography and Human Ecology of the Russian Academy of Sciences. This book appeared in translation in 1999 as *Neotraditionalism in the Russian North: Indigenous Peoples and the Legacy of Perestroika.* Translated by Bruce Grant. Seattle: University of Washington Press.

Poelzer, Greg. 1995. "Devolution, Constitutional Development, and the Russian North." *Post-Soviet Geography* 36: 204–14.

Poponin, V. I. 1978. "Some Data on Changes in Transport Accessibility of East Siberia." *Soviet Geography: Review and Translation* 19(7): 470–74.

Popova, M. N. 1978. *Yakutskaya ASSR: Administrativno-territorial'noye deleniye* (The Yakut ASSR: Administrative and Territorial Division; in Russian). Yakutsk: Yakutskoye knizhnoye izdatel'stvo.

Popova, Zinaida. 1995. "Djogoon-maany Djarkhan" (Noble Djarkhan; in Yakutian).Village song lyrics. Unpublished.

———. 1996. Personal letter in Yakutian to Bella Bychkova Jordan, from Djarkhan, Sakha, November 25.

———. 1999. Personal letter in Yakutian to the authors, from Djarkhan, November 12.

———. 2000. Personal letter in Yakutian to the authors, from Djarkhan, January 11.

"Premier of Russia Cuts Budget 20%." 1997. *New York Times* 146 (May 22): A1, A8.

Priklonskiy, V. L. 1896. *Letopis' yakutskogo kraya, sostavlennaya po ofitsial'nym i istoricheskim dannym* (Records of the Yakut Region, Compiled on the Basis of Official and Historical Data; in Russian). Krasnoyarsk: Yeniseisk Governor's Administration Press.

"Prirodno-khozyaystvennaya kharakteristika senokossov i pastbish' sovkhoza 'Toybokhoyskiy' Suntarskogo rayona YASSR i meropriyatiya po ikh ispol'zovaniyu i uluchsheniyu" (Natural and Economic Characteristics of Haylands and Pastures of the Toybokhoy Sovkhoz in the Suntar Region of the YASSR, and Suggestions for Their Use and Improvement; in Russian). 1980. Report compiled by the students and faculty of the biology and geography Departments of the Yakut State University, participating in the research expedition to the Suntar region. Document in the archives of the Suntar branch of the Yakut State Committee on Land Use and Reform, Suntar, Sakha.

Prokhorov, A. M. (ed.). 1982. *The Great Soviet Encyclopedia.* 32 vols. New York: Macmillan.

Prosterman, Roy L., and Timothy Hanstad. 1993. "A Fieldwork-Based Appraisal of Individual Peasant Farming in Russia." In Don Van Atta (ed.), *The Farmer Threat: The Political Economy of Agrarian Reform in Post-Soviet Russia.* Boulder, CO: Westview Press, 149–89.

*Random House Unabridged Dictionary.* 1993. "Siberia." 2nd ed. New York: Random House, 1775.

*Raspredeleniye naseleniya Rossii po vladeniyu yazykami* (The Distribution of the Population of Russia on the Basis of Language Spoken; in Russian). 1995. Moscow: Goskomstat Rossii.

Rasputin, Valentin. 1996. *Siberia, Siberia.* Evanston, IL: Northwestern University Press.

Remezov, Semyon V. 1958. *The Atlas of Siberia by Semyon V. Remezov.* Edited by Leo Bagrow. The Hague, Netherlands: Mouton. Originally drawn 1697.

Reston, R. 1975. *Aftermath to Revolution: The Soviet Collective Farm.* London: Collier Macmillan.

Robinson, Gerold T. 1949. *Rural Russia under the Old Regime.* New York: Macmillan.

Rodgers, Allan (ed.). 1990. *The Soviet Far East: Geographical Perspectives on Development.* London: Routledge.

*Rossiyskiy Statisticheskiy Ezhegodnik (Russian Statistical Yearbook; in Russian).* 1997. Moscow: Goskomstat Rossii.

"Russia: Eastern Part." 1996. Map, 1:4,000,000. Munich and Stuttgart: Reise- und Verkehrsverlag. Text is in German.

"Russia's Regions: Fiefs and Chiefs." 1997. *The Economist* 342(8001) (January 25): 46–47.

Sakha Republic. 1995a. *Sotsial'no-ekonomicheskoye polozheniye Respubliki Sakha (Yakutiya) za yanvar'-sentyabr' 1995-go goda* (Social-Economic Situation of the Sakha Republic [Yakutia] for January–September 1995; in Russian). Yakutsk: State Committee of Statistics.

———. 1995b. *Ulusy i goroda Respubliki Sakha (Yakutiya) v yanvare-sentyabre 1995-go goda* (Regions and cities of Sakha Republic [Yakutia] for January–September 1995; in Russian). Yakutsk: State Committee of Statistics.

———. 1996. *Trud i zanyatost' v Respublike Sakha (Yakutia) v 1995-om godu* (Labor and Employment in Sakha Republic [Yakutia] in 1995; in Russian). Yakutsk: State Committee of Statistics.

Sallnow, John. 1989. "The Soviet Far East: A Report on Urban and Rural Settlement and Population Change, 1966–1989." *Soviet Geography* 30: 670–83.

Savvinova, Liya N. 1997. Personal letter in Yakutian to Bella Bychkova Jordan December 27, from Suntar, Sakha.

Schmemann, Serge. 1997. *Echoes of a Native Land: Two Centuries of a Russian Village.* New York: Alfred A. Knopf.

Schwarz, Gabriele. 1961. *Allgemeine Siedlungsgeographie.* Berlin: Walter de Gruyter.

Selm, Bert van. 1998. "Economic Performance in Russia's Regions." *Europe-Asia Studies* 50: 603–18.

Semple, Ellen C. 1911. *Influences of Geographic Environment.* New York: Henry Holt.

Semyonov, Yuri. 1944. *The Conquest of Siberia: An Epic of Human Passions.* London: G. Routledge.

Sergeev, G. M. 1989. "Klimat" (Climate). In *Atlas Sel'skogo Khozyaystva Yakutskoy ASSR* (Agricultural Atlas of the Yakut ASSR; in Russian). 1989. Moscow: Glavnoye upravleniye Geodeziye i Kartografiye pri Sovete Ministrov SSSR, 92–96.

Seroshevsky, V. 1993. *Yakuty* (The Yakuts; in Russian). 2nd ed. Moscow: "Nauka."

Seroshevsky, V., and W. G. Sumner. 1901. "The Yakuts." *Journal of the Royal Anthropological Institute of Great Britain and Ireland* 31: 65–110.

Shaw, Denis J. B. (ed.). 1995. *The Post-Soviet Republics: A Systematic Geography.* Harlow, England: Longman.

———. 1999. *Russia in the Modern World: A New Geography.* Oxford, England: Blackwell.

Sheehy, Ann. 1986. "Racial Disturbances in Yakutsk." *Radio Liberty Research Bulletin,* 251: 1–5.

Shubnikova, O. N. 1967. "Resources of Fur-Bearing and Game Animals in Yakutia and Their Utilization." *Soviet Geography: Review and Translation* 8: 793–99.

Shunkov, V. I. 1981. "Geographical Distribution of Siberian Agriculture in the 17th Century." *Soviet Geography: Review and Translation* 22(9): 598–614.

Sidorov, E. I. 1984. "Etnonim Sakha" (The Ethnic Name Sakha; in Russian). In R. Djarylgasinov and V. Nikonov (eds.), *Etnicheskaya Onomastika.* Moscow: "Nauka."

Sivtsev, D. K. (ed.). 1992. *Yakutsk v bylye gody, XVII–XIX vv.* (*Yakutsk in the Past, Seventeenth to Nineteenth Centuries; in Russian*). Yakutsk: Kniga Society.

Sivtsev, Ivan. 1997., interview by the authors of the Sakha Republic minister for agriculture at Mokhsogollokh, Sakha, June 27.

Skryabin, P. N. 1998. "Monitoring Ground-Temperature Conditions in Central Sakha." *Polar Geography* 22: 192–200.

Sleptsov, P. A. 1990. *Izuchayuschim yakutskiy yazyk.* (*For Those Who Study the Yakut Language; in Russian*). Yakutsk: Yakutsk Publishing House.

Slezkine, Yuri. 1994. *Arctic Mirrors: Russia and the Small Peoples of the North.* Ithaca, NY: Cornell University Press.

Specter, Michael. 1998. "A Promised Land of Frozen Milk and Honey." *New York Times* (February 8): W1.

"SSSR/RSFSR/Yakutskaya ASSR." 1980–82. Topographic map quadrangle series, 1:100,000; the sheets named "Arylaks," "El'gyay," "Sardanga," "Suntar," "Tenkaya," and "Toybokhoy," declassified 1993 and available with updated annotations, at the Institute for Land Reform, Suntar, Sakha. Moscow: Akademiya Nauk SSSR. Text is in Russian.

Stavrakis, Peter J., Joan DeBardeleben, and Larry Black (eds.). 1997. *Beyond the Monolith: The Emergence of Regionalism in Post-Soviet Russia.* Baltimore, MD: Johns Hopkins University Press.

Stenin, P. von. 1897. "Das Haus der Jakuten (Ostsibirien)." *Globus* 72: 344–47.

Strahlenberg, Philip J. von. 1738. *An Historico-Geographical Description of the North and Eastern Parts of Europe and Asia, But More Particularly of Russia, Siberia, and Great Tartary.* London: J. Brotherton.

Stuart, Robert C. 1972. *The Collective Farm in Soviet Agriculture.* Lexington, MA: Lexington Books.

——— (ed.). 1984. *The Soviet Rural Economy.* Totowa, NJ: Rowman and Allanheld.

Suslov, S. P. 1961. *Physical Geography of Asiatic Russia.* San Francisco: W. H. Freeman.

Symons, Leslie. 1972. *Russian Agriculture: A Geographic Survey.* London: Bell and Sons.

Tikhomirov, Vladimir. 1997. "Food Balance in the Russian Far East." *Polar Geography* 21: 155–202.

Tikhonova, Aleksandra. 1996. Native and resident of Djarkhan, interviewed by the authors, Djarkhan, Sakha, July 18.

Tikhonova, Tanya. 1997. Native and resident of Djarkhan, interviewed by the authors, July 8.

Tokarev, S. A., and I. S. Gurvich. 1964. "The Yakuts." In Maksim G. Levin and L. P. Potapov (eds., *The Peoples of Siberia.* Chicago: University of Chicago Press, 243–304.

Torgovkina, T. A. (ed.). 2000. *Respublika Sakha (Yakutiya): Statisticheskiy Spravochnik (Republic of Sakha [Yakutia]: Stastistical Bulletin*, in Russian). Yakutsk: Gaskamstat Rossiyskoy Federatsiy.

Treadgold, Donald W. 1957. *The Great Siberian Migration*. Princeton, NJ: Princeton University Press.

Tuan, Yi-fu. 1974. *Topophilia*. Englewood Cliffs, NJ: Prentice-Hall.

———. 1976. "Geopiety: A Theme in Man's Attachment to Nature and to Place." In David Lowenthal and Martyn J. Bowden (eds.), *Geographies of the Mind*. New York: Oxford University Press, 11–39.

———. 1980. "Rootedness and Sense of Place." *Landscape* 24: 3–8.

Vil'chek, G. Y., L. R. Serebryannyy, and A. A. Tishkov. 1996. "A Geographic Perspective on Sustainable Development in the Russian Arctic." *Polar Geography* 20: 249–66.

Vinogradova, V. V. 1997. "Impact of Global Warming on Climatic Severity in Northern and Eastern Russia During the 1980s." *Polar Geography* 21: 70–77.

Vinokurova, Uliana Alekseevna. 1994. *Skaz o narode Sakha (Legends of the Yakuts;* in Russian). Yakutsk: "Bichik."

Vitebsky, Piers. 1989. "Reindeer Herders of Northern Yakutia." *Polar Record* 25: 213–18.

———. 1990. "Yakut." In Graham E. Smith (ed.), *The Nationalities Question in the Soviet Union*. London: Longman, 304–19.

———. 1996. "The Northern Minorities." In Graham E. Smith (ed.), *The Nationalities Question in the Post-Soviet States*. London: Longman, 94–112.

Vorob'yev, V. V. 1975. "The Settling of Eastern Siberia before the Revolution." *Soviet Geography: Review and Translation* 16(2): 75–85.

Vrutzevich, M. S. 1891. "Obitatyeli kul'tura i zhizn' v Yakutskoy oblasti" (Culture and Life of the People of the Yakutsk Territory; in Russian). *Zapiski Imperatorskago Russkago Geograficheskago Obshchestva po Otdeleniyu Etnografii* 17(2): 1–41.

Walter, Eugene V. 1988. *Placeways: A Theory of the Human Environment*. Chapel Hill: University of North Carolina Press.

Wein, Norbert. 1991. "Jakutien und die Problematik des sibirischen Nordens." *Die Erde* 122: 191–207.

———. 1997. "Jakutien (Republik Sacha)." *Zeitschrift für Wirtschaftsgeographie* 41: 123–32.

Wein, Norbert, and Ivan Egorov. 1992. "Wirtschafts- und Lebensverhältnisse im subpolaren Sibirien (das Beispiel Nordostjakutien)." *Petermanns Geographische Mitteilungen* 136(5/6): 251–66.

Wescott, Gary, and Monika Wescott. 1997a. "The Road of Bones to the Coldest Place in the World." *Russian Life* 40(3): 12–21.

———. 1997b. "Winter Roads of Siberia." *Russian Life* 40(4): 24–29.

Wieczynski, Joseph L. 1976. *The Russian Frontier: The Impact of Borderlands on the Course of Early Russian History*. Charlottesville, VA: University Press of Virginia.

Williams, Daniel. 1997. "Creating a Hot Property in Siberia Is Every Bit as Hard as It Sounds." *Washington Post* (October 3): A29, A34.

Wines, Michael. 1998. "Siberians' Coming Winter: Hungry, Cold and Broke." *New York Times* (October 21): A1, A10.

Wixman, Ronald. 1984. *The People of the U.S.S.R.: An Ethnographic Handbook*. Armonk, NY: M. E. Sharpe.

Wood, Alan (ed.). 1987. *Siberia: Problems and Prospects for Regional Development*. London: Croom Helm.

Wood, Alan, and R. A. French (eds.). 1989. *The Development of Siberia: People and Resources*. London: Macmillan.

Yakovlev, Arkady. 1997. Interview by the authors with research assistant, Suntar Ulus regional archives, Suntar, Sakha, July 15.

Yakovlev, Georgiy. 1997. Interview of the governor of Suntar Ulus by the authors, at Suntar, Sakha, July 15.

"Yakutskaya ASSR." 1934. Map, 1:2,000,000, sheet 3: "Leno-Vilyuiskiy krai." Moscow: Akademiya Nauk SSSR, Izdaniye Vsesoyuznogo Kartograficheskogo Tresta GGU-NKTP SSSR.

Yegorova, Svetlana. 1994–95. "Yakutia—Siberia's Chernobyl." *Sibirica: The Journal of Siberian Studies* 1(2): 35–37.

"Zapisi novogo sel'skokhozyaystvennogo kooperativa Djarkhana" (Records of the New Agricultural Cooperative of Djarkhan; in Russian). 1993–97. Records in the village council hall, Djarkhan, Sakha.

# INDEX

BELLA BYCHKOVA JORDAN, a native of Djarkhan, Siberia, formerly worked in the diplomatic protocol office and international department of the Ministry of Foreign Relations of the Republic of Sakha/Yakutia, Russia. A recipient of the Lenin Prize, the most prestigious graduate scholarship in the Soviet Union, she studied linguistics in Moscow and now is a doctoral candidate in cultural geography at the University of Texas.

TERRY G. JORDAN-BYCHKOV holds the Walter Prescott Webb Chair in the Department of Geography at the University of Texas at Austin. He is a past president of the Association of American Geographers, and his numerous publications (including thirteen books) have won major awards.